# HITTING THE TURF

David Ashforth was a student of history at Cambridge from 1968 to 1971, where he divided his time between the University library and the betting shop. When not going to the races, he has been a lecturer in modern history, looked after laboratory rats, and written papers on strategic quality management. He is now the *Sporting Life's* senior reporter and columnist.

# Hitting
# The Turf

## *A Punting Life*

### David Ashforth

**HEADLINE**

First published in 1996
by HEADLINE BOOK PUBLISHING

First published in paperback in 1997
by HEADLINE BOOK PUBLISHING

10 9 8 7 6 5 4 3 2 1

ISBN 0 7472 5321 8

Typeset by
Letterpart Limited, Reigate, Surrey

Printed and bound in Great Britain by
Cox & Wyman Ltd, Reading, Berks

HEADLINE BOOK PUBLISHING
A division of Hodder Headline PLC
338 Euston Road
London NW1 3BH

# Hitting
# The Turf

*A Punting Life*

# Contents

# *Introduction*

## Lining Up

I love racing. Or do I? How can you love racing when Judge Jeffreys has just examined a photograph with a magnifying glass and decided, in his infinite malice, that the horse you backed was the thickness of the £10 note you're never going to see again behind the one you almost backed but didn't?

I love racing: a sport in which a small animal sits on a large one and shouts 'goonyubugger' until the pair of them have caught up with a wooden stick known as the winning post. With some horses, usually the ones you have backed, it can take an awfully long time.

Traditionally, lovers of horse racing have a passion for shooting pheasants, hunting foxes, serving in the army, having double-barrelled surnames, and wearing trilbies, but not everyone who likes racing has killed someone. Some people fall for racing because they love horses. Horses are beautiful creatures. There they stand, staring imperiously into the distance, ears pricked, and we fall in love with them. We marvel at how majestic they look and wonder what they are

1

thinking. They aren't thinking anything.

Then there are the gamblers, drawn into racing through a shop door which leads to a counter with a sign over it which reads 'Bet Here'. And they do, even though there are three counters which say 'Bet Here' and only one which says 'Pay-Out'. I like gamblers. I always have done. I like the way they don't know what the rate of interest is on savings accounts and I like the way they look forward to the 3.30 at Catterick despite what happened in the 2.45 at Yarmouth. I like the way they give up gambling for good at the end of Tuesday afternoon and don't have another bet until Wednesday. I liked betting on horses as soon as I tried it, thirty years ago in a smoky betting shop in Borehamwood High Street. I loved it when I went to Sandown Park on Len's Lambretta and watched Lester Piggott win on Italiano. Over the years, I have liked it so much that there has hardly been time to fit in anything else, and although I have done all I can to help the bookmakers, I wish I could have done more.

I probably would have done, if I'd branched out into greyhounds. Len and I went to Walthamstow a few times, but somehow my interest never survived Portsmouth. That evening, whichever one it was, Len and I were in a dreadful state; the sort you only get into when you think you might miss the first race. We'd worked out our strategy and, when we finally got there, I dashed up to the Tote window and said, breathlessly, 'Six and five, reversed.' The Tote lady produced a look of utter contempt. 'There are only five traps,' she said. After that, I stuck to the horses.

It's so easy. All you have to do is find your way to a racecourse, put your hand in your back pocket (unless someone else has got there before you), and pass the contents to a man called Jolly Jim. He gives you a small piece of cardboard which, after a decent interval, you throw away. When you put your hand in your pocket and find there is nothing there, you stop. It's a good system, and I followed it diligently for many years, until my bank informed me that they could see no future in it. Then I started writing about it.

# The Punter's Glossary

**Accumulator:** Bet requiring punter to make additional selections until one loses.

**Ante-post:** Special arrangement under which punters are allowed to lose their money six months before the race has started.

**Any-to-come:** No.

**Betting shop:** Place for depositing your money. In that respect, similar to a bank.

**Betting slip:** Piece of paper or card, costing between £1 and £10,000, useful for rolling cigarettes.

**Blinker:** The first act of desperation (*see also* **hood**, **visor**, **gelding**, **put down**).

**Bookmaker:** Wealthy victim of repeated misfortune.

**Chase:** Race in which the horse you have backed falls over. A technique for enlarging the hole you have been digging.

**Double:** Bet based on the erroneous conviction that it is possible to pick more than one winner in the same afternoon.

**Dual forecast:** Bet involving two selections, A and B, in which A finishes first and B third, or B finishes first and A third.

**Each way:** Opportunity to lose twice in one bet.

**Favourite:** Horse held in high regard by bookmakers.

**Form book:** Historical work, useful for predicting what will happen in the past.

**Gap:** Something jockeys imagine they have seen. A space comfortably big enough for two chocolate fingers.

**Goliath:** Tremendously large bet, with the same outcome as the original.

**Good thing:** Losing horse.

**Horse:** Magnificent creature with no sense of justice.

**Inspection:** Examination of course to see whether it is fit for you to lose your money on.

**Jockey:** Small person employed by trainer to ruin your win double.

**Jockey Club:** High-class mortuary.

**Ladbrokes:** Organisation for removing money from people's pockets (*see* **punter**).

**Last show:** Number larger than the starting price.

**Levy Board:** Organisation set up to try and get some money out of Ladbrokes.

**Off:** Term used to describe a horse's eighth run of the season.

**Punter:** Person with no money.

**Racecourse:** Place for seeing, at first hand, where things go wrong.

**Rails:** Railings with spikes on them provided for the benefit of punters wishing to impale themselves, as in, 'He's on the rails at Ascot'.

**Starter:** Official who drops a flag to indicate that hope has ended and experience is about to begin.

**Steward:** Official employed to disabuse you of the belief that you have just backed your first winner for five weeks.

**Straight forecast:** Bet involving two selections, A and B, in which B finishes first and A second.

**Trainer:** Keeper of domestic animals.

**Union Jack:** Bet in which punters demonstrate their patriotism by making a contribution to Her Majesty's Exchequer.

**Unlucky:** Horses that took part in a race but did not win it.

**Whip:** Stick used to make a horse go faster than it wants to. Jockeys sometimes use it too much, except when they are riding one you have backed, when they don't use it enough (*see* **insufficiently thrashed**).

**Winning post:** Wooden stick inserted in the ground in the wrong place.

# Chapter One

## Learning Bad Habits

The accelerator cable on Len's Lambretta had broken, so I sat on the back holding the bare wire: when Len twisted the handlebar to change gear I let the cable go slack, and then pulled it taut again as he went from second, to third, to top.

We went into the cheap enclosure in the middle of Sandown Park and stood against the white running rail, not far from the winning post. You couldn't see a lot from there, but for the first time I heard the noise of galloping hooves, the whips and shouts and rub of leather driving for the finish. Just beyond the rail, a touch away, we glimpsed the skewed ferocity of Lester Piggott, on Italiano, reaching for the winning post. We were there: part of this special world.

I'd had a bet on Lester, placed after walking nervously along a line of bookmakers, with their boards and chalk and big, open bags, shouting through gaps between their rotten teeth. '11–8 the field! 11–8 this good thing!'

'Two shillings on Italiano, please.'

The willing and peering during the race, the steam rising from the straining horses, the urgings of their jockeys, the shouting of the crowd, the suspense of the finish and photo-finish, the elation of – 'First, number two.' This was for me.

While we were waiting for the next race, Len and I walked across towards the sprint finish, in the centre of the track, and watched a three-card trickster ply his dishonourable trade. A small man whipped up a lightweight table with a top about one foot square. Folded up, like a deckchair, it could be carried easily, and quickly, under one arm. Lightning fast, the dealer spread three cards face down on the table. One of the three cards was a queen. All you had to do was find the lady. He slid the cards back into his hands and spread them out again.

The dealer didn't work alone, and later I realised how easy it was to pick out his accomplices. They were his first audience, drawing in another audience, tempting passing punters with a hubbub of voices and a show of banknotes. The tricksters played on the curiosity aroused by a huddle of figures gathered around something that couldn't quite be seen without stopping, and stepping closer, and becoming part of the action. Some members of the gang loitered on the outer fringes of the crowd, drawing in the waverers. Others banged their bank-notes on to one of the three cards and, behold, the Queen of Hearts. Twenty pounds down, twenty pounds handed over by the dealer, good as gold.

The gang had an eye for the weak and gullible and they caressed and cajoled them into drawing their money out of their pockets and, finally, on to one of the restless cards. Getting it out of their pockets, that was the thing. They had ploys. The card sharp would look away while the victim's new buddy picked up a card and made as if to mark it with his teeth. Then he would drag the innocent's hand over to a card on the table, whispering 'Hold it there, mate,' conspiratorially, as he peeled off £30 and slapped the notes on to the card. There's our lady. The dealer, easy-going as could be, paid the buddy, who turned to his new friend and whispered again, 'Go on, mate, that's the one.' But when Len put £10 on the card, it wasn't the one; and if it had been, they wouldn't have paid him. 'Not yet, sir, not ready yet sir' – with just a glance of menace, a nicely judged measure of intimidation.

That day at Sandown a punter kicked over the brittle table as the truth and his own naïvety dawned on him. The card sharp, the table, the gang all melted away and two policemen strolled across the grass in the sunshine, too late.

Most of the time Len and I didn't go to the racecourse. Instead, after school, we dashed off to a betting shop in Borehamwood High Street. I was seventeen when I first pushed my hand between the coloured strips of plastic which hung in that doorway. The shop was smoky and mysterious, seedy and forbidden: irresistible.

Len and I had a system. It was based on Lester Piggott. The first thing you did was work out how much you wanted to win. We decided £2. Then you put whatever needed to be put on Lester Piggott's next mount, at the quoted odds, to win £2. If it won, you started again. If it didn't, you put enough on Lester's next ride to win £2 plus what you had already lost. When he had ridden seven losers in a row, and the eighth won, we heaved a sigh of relief, and stopped. We had spotted a slight flaw in the system. If Lester's eighth mount had lost, we wouldn't have had any money left to back number nine.

After that, every Saturday, I did a yankee, to a one-shilling stake: four horses combined in six doubles, four trebles and a four-horse accumulator. On 29 April 1967 Fresh Scotch went in at 50–1 and Easter Island joined him at 15–2. Len and I scootered off to Borehamwood High Street and picked up £21 13s 6d. It seemed like a fortune. It was a fortune. We bought two tins of Nestlé's sweetened milk and walked down the High Street sucking it through the holes we had punched in the lids. That lovely, syrupy, sickly, sweetened milk – I expect it's illegal now.

Before long, when the morning newspapers arrived at school, the first page I turned to was the racing page – unless Doncaster Rovers had played the previous night, in which case I turned to the football page. When you are young, your senses are sharp: an unfamiliar name, a sequence of form figures, the shades of print on a page are enough to excite, almost to smell. I think it was the *Daily Express* I smelt first. Their tipster put a round, black blob next to his selection. I liked that.

Somewhere on Doncaster racecourse, there's a tree my grandfather planted. I know, because I've seen a newspaper cutting from 1947 with a picture of him planting it. Thomas W. Hibbert, Doncaster Borough's chief electrical engineer. Later, my grandfather used to knit dishcloths on big wooden knitting needles; and after that, he went bald.

My father's father was a miner at Bentley colliery. It was his proud boast that, during the General Strike of 1926, he was one of the ones who stayed out for the full six months. He died when I was three, and it was only much later that an uncle told me that my grandfather sometimes came home on payday, held out his empty hands, and said, 'All gone.'

My grandmother ran a corner shop in Balby, on the edge of Doncaster. She sold sweets in triangular paper bags and butter cut from a big slab, and a wheel went backwards and forwards, slicing ham. Women came in wearing slippers and hairnets, and we thought nothing of it. 'Our Sandra went to Gaumont last night, to see that *Psycho*. She said she were that scared, she almost gave 'usband an 'ug. 'Ave you got a jar of those pickles, luv?' My grandmother didn't believe in self-service, and when the supermarkets came she kept on cutting butter from the big slab, and slicing ham, and going broke. My grandmother's shop in Oswin Avenue is a hairdresser's now, and the Gaumont's a garage.

It was Uncle George, next door on Thompson Avenue, who

introduced me to racing. George made custard pies for the Doncaster Co-op. On Saturday afternoons, he liked to have a few bets on the horses, and we'd watch them on television. Then we'd check his football pools. He got those wrong, too. I never went to Doncaster racecourse, but I sometimes went to Belle Vue football ground on the other side of the road and, years later, I gave Doncaster Rovers a few match balls. I don't know why, because they didn't know what to do with them.

Even before the trip to Sandown Park and the betting shop in Borehamwood High Street, I remember Arkle; a misty, monochrome shape moving across a television screen. I didn't understand what was so special about him; I didn't know what it meant for one horse to give weight away to another. I only knew that, when Arkle's name was mentioned on television, it was in a tone of awe that made me want to watch.

I understand now. Imagine an Olympic sprinter lining up five metres behind the other finalists, and beating them; a golf player forced to tee off for the British Open with a four-stroke penalty, and still winning. That is how good Arkle was. It was Arkle who forced the Irish handicapper to extend the handicap, so that he could be made to concede enough weight to give his opponents a chance; Arkle who was odds-on to win the 1965 Whitbread Gold Cup under the awesome weight of 12st 7lb, and won it; Arkle who twice won the Hennessy Gold Cup carrying the same weight, and failed to complete the hat-trick only because he could not quite give 35lb to Stalbridge Colonist, a top-class chaser who, four months later, was narrowly beaten in the Cheltenham Gold Cup. Arkle won the same Gold Cup, chasing's blue riband, three times in a row.

Those who watched the 1964 duel between Arkle and the mighty Mill House, a champion in his own right, will never forget the moment when Willie Robinson raised his despairing whip on Mill House, when Arkle quickened, and every doubter knew that all the claims were true. Here was a horse a whole generation would say to their dying day, was the best chaser they had ever seen. Arkle didn't need to be driven hard to give his best, he gave it freely. Looking at the old films again, what is striking is Arkle's willingness. He raced as if he wanted to win, stretching athletically for the line. He was the first horse I really wanted to win, even when I hadn't backed him.

In January 1968 I got a job on the production line at Vauxhall, in Luton. Mostly, I worked nights. I liked night shifts: the pleasing oddness of working at two in the morning; having the afternoons free. To begin with, I fitted hinges to car doors. I worked with a big West Indian. 'Were you courting at the weekend?', he'd ask, every Monday, and then wink a lecherous wink and smile a big, rotten-toothed smile. He had a 1000 cc motorbike and sometimes gave me a lift home, when we'd break the 100 m.p.h. barrier down the A6. It was an exhilarating feeling, like flying over a jump on a horse. Another friend let me try out his bike, but I took a corner too fast and the bike went down, and so did we, in a long slide across the road. The man in the car behind stopped, which was kind of him. He was an off-duty policeman. I got banned for three months, and I didn't get to ride a motorbike again.

At Vauxhall, I graduated from fitting hinges to drilling holes in the car bodies where the metal trim went. You pushed the drill on to the end of a long, snaking air-hose; then you fixed one of the jigs to the car and drilled through the holes in the jig. After breaking a lot of drills, I moved on to bonnets. It was a tough job, fitting bonnets. The track moved steadily on, and on, and on. If you took too long, you disappeared into the next section. As I drifted past, the foreman would shake his head and raise his eyebrows and say, 'You haven't got it, have you, son?' And I'd shout back, 'No, but I'm sure it's in here somewhere.'

Now and again, when the moon was blue, a nervous team of

managers would appear on the shop floor. We stood and stared at them, these strange, unfamiliar animals, and then they were gone, scuttling back upstairs into the safety of their offices. The word went round that someone had been sent from America to sort things out, and soon afterwards the track speeded up. Men took it in turns to drop a tool into the gap in the middle of the track. It was nice when it shuddered to a halt. We'd sit down and get our sandwiches out.

Len and I made occasional forays to the races: to Newmarket, where we had our first experience of inside information, and to Alexandra Park, where we had our first experience of Alexandra Park's starting arrangements.

It was Cambridgeshire day when we went to Newmarket, parked Len's scooter, and looked for a betting shop. We couldn't find a shop, but we managed to find a hovel, with a till on a shaky counter and wallpaper painted nicotine brown. Scraps of paper hung from nails banged into the walls. We unhooked a few pieces, wrote out our bets, and handed them to a man who was busy dropping ash on to the counter.

'What's your name?' he asked. Why was he asking? Did he suspect that I was only seventeen? Was he a police informer?

'Why do you want to know?' I replied.

'If we don't know your name, we don't know whose bet it is, do we?'

They didn't issue receipts; they just took names. So I made one up. It didn't matter, because we didn't need to go back again.

As we went down a narrow lane to collect the scooter, we passed a small, stocky man leading a horse. It was the nearest either of us had ever been to a racehorse. We got talking, and before long the man became conspiratorial, as people with racehorses do. 'Murless has got one today,' he said, looking round for eavesdroppers, and motioning us to lower our heads into a secret circle. 'Love For Sale.' Here was the new thrill of a tip; and not just a tip, but a real tip, from a man in the know, a man with a horse.

He gave us another tip, for the Cambridgeshire, but it wasn't Dites, who won at 33–1, nor Isis, who finished second, at 40–1, and our confidence was shaken by the time Love For Sale ran in the Houghton Stakes. Still, we backed her at 4–1, and Lester got Noel Murless's filly home by a short head, bless his heart; starting price 11–4. Maybe the man with the horse did know something.

The decor at Alexandra Park reminded us a bit of the Newmarket betting shop. The track was the real curiosity, though: it was shaped like a frying pan, and it was important to have your horse lined up properly for the journey up the handle. In those days, starting stalls were things foreigners had. Real racing countries (Britain) used a proper system of tapes and flags operated by men who still called themselves 'Major', even though they'd left the army twenty years ago. The system worked pretty well. The ones who were trying lined up at the front and started as quickly as they could, while the ones who weren't mooched around at the back. The day we went, Len backed Willow Red in the apprentice race. As the tapes went up, so did Ray Still, leaving Willow Red on his own, several feet underneath him. It was difficult to ride a start from up there, let alone a finish.

In those days, the officials used to have terrible trouble with the equipment, especially their eyes. A month after Ray Still had been rescued by a fire-engine, the judge at Newcastle confidently declared that Tant Pis had won the Crumstone Handicap Chase. Half an hour later, when a photograph of the finish was pinned up on the notice board, someone pointed out that there seemed to be another horse ahead of Tant Pis. The judge took another look, and confidently declared Moidore's Token the winner. By then, however, the jockeys had weighed in and bets had to be settled on the judge's original verdict.

I remember it happening again, at Carlisle in 1973. Ian Johnson, a young apprentice, rode a peach of a race to land the spoils on Brass Farthing, only to be told by the judge that Brother Somers had beaten him. Driving home, depressed, Johnson heard an announcement on the car radio. The judge had got the horses' numbers mixed up, and Brass Farthing had indeed won; but it was too late to save the punters who had backed him. 'Not a Brass Farthing for winner backers,' read the *Sporting Life*'s headline.

At the end of May 1968 Len and I set off on the scooter again, this time for Epsom. The accelerator cable had been repaired, but the flywheel hadn't, so I carried a brick in my duffel-coat pocket to unjam it. I don't like Epsom. Just when you think you're almost there, it moves another five miles away. When we finally arrived on the Downs, a man who looked as if he'd fallen on hard times and been impaled on them came up to us with a racecard. What it boiled down to was this. Either we gave him the price of his next Derby Day drink, or we didn't. He had prepared for the latter eventuality by collecting a large reserve of spittle in his mouth. Len told the man what he could do with his racecard and the man told Len that he was going to rip his head off and stuff it up his backside. Then he was going to kill him.

The next thing I remember is standing in front of a book-maker taking evens about Sir Ivor. It was a shrewd investment: an even £2 about a 5–4 on shot. At Epsom, in the days when they had crowds there, you couldn't watch the Derby from the Downs. Hats, scarves, elbows, binoculars, heads – you saw lots of those, but not horses. Instead, you absorbed the Derby through snatched glimpses of the race and the sounds of the crowd. That's how I remember Sir Ivor, in exciting, half-seen, distant glimpses. I wanted him to win so much, but as they headed down the finishing straight all I could see, like frames from a film, was Connaught, out on his own. They would never catch him. I craned vainly for Sir Ivor's colours: chocolate with pale blue hoops and a pale blue cap. They were nowhere. Then the commentator's half-heard voice, and an answering roar from the crowd and, suddenly, a glimpse of chocolate and blue and Lester Piggott asking as only he could. But the gap was too big, the post too near; and then came Sir Ivor's electrifying burst and everyone was shouting and Lester easing to the finish. Afterwards, I remember unjamming the flywheel with the brick.

That June I walked up the gangway on to a ship at Southampton and sailed for New York. On the way, we met a force nine gale. There seemed to be fewer passengers every day. They were there, somewhere, but not for dinner. I sat in the deserted lounge and read *The Lord of the Rings*. For three months, I hitched around the East Coast and Mid-West, staying with people I met. It was 1968 and I was nineteen. Bliss. I went to the Newport Jazz Festival and fished for sea bass off Rhode Island. I slept out by Niagara Falls and watched people burn their draft cards in a park in Boston. I saw Tracy dance with a snake under the strobe lights; and Chalyce stood at the top of the stairs and sang songs from *Hair*, and gave me *The Old Man and the Sea*. We all smoked pot and talked about Vietnam and played The Doors, and I forgot about horses.

Emmanuel College awarded me the Gerald Campbell Owen Scholarship in History, and in return, at a special dinner, I tried to read something in Latin from the back of a wooden table-tennis bat.

When I arrived at Cambridge in October 1968 for the start of the academic year, the first thing I did was look for a betting shop. I've never known a place like it for the lack of them. I walked the streets until my feet hurt before I finally found one in King Street, next to a barber's shop. It's gone now, and so has my need for a barber. I spent a lot of time in that betting shop, and when it moved further down the same street, I spent a lot of time there, instead. It was in that spartan den that I first met Ian Carnaby, who has been a friend ever since. Twenty-five years later, Ian and I were both writing for the *Sporting Life* and realising that maybe we couldn't make it pay, after all.

During the afternoon, we used to stand inside with the *Life* spread out on the formica tops; and after 6.30 p.m., when the shop had to close, we stood outside and listened to the Extel commentary through the window. I never thought I'd miss those commentaries, but I do. They were comfortingly familiar, and so was the phrase one regular insisted on shouting out.

'They're under starter's orders,' announced the Extel man.

'Get your knickers off!'

'And they're off.'

I used to fold my betting slip in two. In the bottom left-hand corner, I wrote the number of the horse. To the right of that, I'd write the betting shows. In the bottom right-hand corner, I'd put the number of runners. Along the top edge, if it was a Flat race, I'd mark off the furlongs, and during the commentary I'd write down the horse's position as the race unfolded through Extel's well-worn phrases and my imagination. I was still doing it in 1987, when televisions finally arrived in betting shops.

The King Street shop contained some memorable chunks of life's flotsam and jetsam. There was a man with a thick East European accent who said he had fought for the Yugoslav royalists against Tito's communists. He had a painting which the soldiers had pillaged from an art gallery. It was an important picture, worth a lot of money, he said, but he was frightened to sell it, or show it to anyone, including me. And there was Fred, one of the regulars: an old man and rather vague, but one day he won £900. We were all pleased for him. Fred went into the toilet at the back of the shop with all the banknotes in an envelope. He left the envelope in the toilet, and when he went back later to get it, it had gone.

Someone suggested diving down the toilet but that was a silly idea, because Fred couldn't swim.

## Chapter Two

# Sausage Rolls and Obituaries

The cover is speckled brown now, but I haven't thrown it away. 'Gedenkschrift Martin Gohring – Franz Steiner Verlag GmBH. Wiesbaden. 1968.' I don't know what it means, either, but one of the contributions is called 'The Nobility and Revolution in Mainz, 1792–1793. Von T. C. W. Blanning.' During my first year at Cambridge, I used to go to Sidney Sussex College for tutorials in modern European history with Dr Blanning. The first time I went, a photograph on the ledge above the fireplace caught my eye. 'That's Ron Sheather, isn't it?', I asked. Sheather was not a well-known jockey, and the French Revolution went much more smoothly after that. When Blakeney finished second in the 1969 Lingfield Derby Trial, Dr Blanning assured me that he would win the Derby. 'He's the only one certain to stay,' he said, blunt with confidence; and he was right.

In those days, though, I was keener on jump racing than the Flat. I rarely went to Newmarket but Jeff Connor, another betting-shop habitué, and I rarely missed a meeting at Huntingdon. It was there, early in December 1970, that we first saw K. Payne. Anubis had just won the selling hurdle (it was always a selling hurdle), with N. Mackness on board. We stood and watched K. Payne in the winner's enclosure, and wondered who Mrs T. Wade, the owner, was. When you first start following racing, all the small trainers, jockeys and owners are just initials. You pick up their full names later, if at all. K. for Ken Payne, N. for Norman Mackness, T. for Thelma Wade.

'Window' Payne, once a window cleaner, didn't make any bones about the kind of trainer he was. 'My destiny was to be a gambling trainer,' he wrote when he was one no longer. 'I was hanging in there. I was scheming. I think I must have been born scheming. A good winner, that's all I needed. One good coup to clout the bookmakers around their earholes.' At the races, Payne had a nasty habit of wearing those over-smart, over-tight suits with all the accessories spiv-smart. He used to pay a man called Lino Tobias, or something similar, to make his fingernails look like a million dollars, which was roughly how much Lino charged.

Payne started training at Sherfield English, on the edge of the New Forest, in 1967. To begin with, he had a few selling platers, and to end with, he had a lot of selling platers. Payne didn't think there was much to the job of getting horses fit, so he left most of that to his head lad. His own special system for training horses was an unusual one, picked up while doing National Service in Kuala Lumpur, between bouts of tropical diseases. It involved injecting anabolic steroids into horses' necks.

Away from the stables, Payne got on with the serious business of pulling the birds and any potential owners who happened to be in the 21 Club in Mayfair, or Bentley's Oyster Bar. He went in looking like Tommy Steele and came out with an unlikely collection of owners, among them the Queen's dress designer Sir Norman Hartnell, Max Bygraves, Stanley Baker and Larry Parnes. Krishna Maharaj, who sold yams, was so impressed by Payne that one day in 1971 he drove up to his yard in a Rolls-Royce bearing the registration number KM1 and insisted on buying Berkeley House in Lambourn for Payne to train from. Things didn't work out terribly well for Payne, but they worked out a lot worse for Maharaj, who ended up on death row in Florida, convicted of having killed two business-men in a Miami hotel. A lot of Payne's owners were a bit unusual. Chummy Gaventa vetoed one carefully planned coup because it clashed with a Jewish holiday, and Tom Umpleby scuppered another because he thought Kithairon, Payne's best horse, might like half a gallon of yoghurt for his tea.

According to Payne, the air at Lambourn was 'thick with envy, with bitterness, with hate, with social climbing of the most outrageous sort. A year of it was enough for me.' So he moved north, to Kingsley House in Middleham, Yorkshire. At his peak, which didn't last long, Payne had over a hundred horses in training. He was the king of sellers, and took to entering seven or eight of them in the same race. He said he did it to confuse other people but in the end it had him fooled, too.

In 1976, financially posthumous, Payne took an overdose of malaria tablets. He chose malaria tablets because they couldn't kill you but, to be on the safe side, he moved to London to be comforted by Mandy Perrement, a seventeen-year-old model. When he came round, he wrote an extraordinary book, called *The Coup*. It's a book you pick up and read in one sitting, and it was probably written in the same way. There are some tremendous mistakes in it, including a particularly fine one in the description of Payne's first successful gamble, at Catterick early in 1968: 'Brian Fletcher got him out of the stalls sharply, and as the pack reached the first hurdle, Neronton was tucked in neatly behind the favourite.' They don't have stalls in jump races.

Payne added a vivid dose of colour to the racing scene, but he left a trail of disaster behind him which made a large dent in his popularity: bills unpaid, wages unpaid, horses unfed, wives and children unsatisfied.

After I had been writing about racing for a while, and had worked my way through most of the characters I really wanted to write about, Payne was one of the two still left on the list. The other was Arthur Stephenson, for years the top northern trainer, and canny as a lock. John Banks, the best-known race-course bookmaker of his day, used to have horses with Stephenson, but took them away, which was unusual, because there weren't many better trainers. When Banks was asked why he had done it, he replied: 'Arthur's unlucky for me and he drives me mad. He's got some dreadful habits. He'll walk up to you, pinch your cheeks, ruffle your hair and say, "Hello, how are you?"

'If you've got a horse with him and it loses, he'll walk up to you and say, "You shouldn't have backed it, John. You shouldn't back horses and you shouldn't take even money about them."

'I'm a punter and I'll put £1,000 on a 4–1 on chance if I think it's going to bloody win. No, your horse loses and he walks up behind you, knocks your hat over your eyes, knocks your binoculars off your shoulders and then says, "You shouldn't have backed that." '

Stephenson didn't give interviews. I'd ring him up now and again and tell him that, sooner or later, he'd have to talk to some bugger, and it might as well be this one; and he'd chuckle, and say, 'Get away, lad.' In the end I wrote him a letter, enclosing a pencil and a piece of paper for him to reply. I told him that if we waited much longer I'd be reading about him in his obituary. He wrote a lovely, funny letter back, saying he hoped it would be my obituary he'd be reading first. We had a few more chuckles on the phone, but I never did get to interview him – only to read his obituary.

I treasured Arthur's letter and, foolishly, put it in a file in my briefcase with another letter I treasured, from Robert Morley. One evening, Ian and I returned to my car between eating at El Greco's and blackjacking at the Victoria Sporting Club to find my car broken into and my briefcase stolen. I didn't mind about the other things they took, but I minded a lot about the letters.

Once or twice I made a serious effort to find Ken Payne. I tracked down one person, then another, and all of them said the same thing. They didn't know where Ken was, but they thought he was in America; so-and-so would know. But so-and-so didn't know. Someone said that Ken had the concession to sell Lexus cars in Florida; but he didn't. Finally, I tracked down Payne's ex-wife, Linda. She wasn't sure herself whether she was his first, second or third wife, but she was certain that they had a son together. That's it, I thought, I'm there. If they share a son, they'll be in touch.

'We didn't hear from him for ten years,' Linda told me, 'and then he suddenly rang up from California and said he'd like to see his son.' So his unworldly fifteen-year-old son flew to Los Angeles, where Ken met him, along with three glamorous girlfriends. According to Linda, not an altogether neutral witness, Ken promptly disappeared, leaving the lad with his girlfriends.

In 1995 I was told that Payne had left the States and was living at Newcastle, near Sydney. Although I found a lot of people, including Mrs T. Wade (in Harley Street) and Mandy Perrement (in America) and Payne's niece (in Australia), I still couldn't find Payne. He was supposed to be on holiday with a speedboat in Western Samoa. I was left with my memory of him standing with Thelma Wade and Anubis in the winner's enclosure at Huntingdon.

In those days, going racing was a real adventure: days of excitement and anticipation beforehand, then a bus from Cambridge, a copy of the *Sporting Life* and a long, chatty walk from Huntingdon town centre to the racecourse, talking about what we were going to back. Once we hitched to Warwick and slept in the bus station, and the next morning got into the race-course for nothing. Mostly, though, we went into the betting shop on King Street where, once or twice a week, I'd do a yankee. The rest of the time, I'd do something else. Until November 1969.

On 15 November I did my usual yankee. Three of them came up. (In yankees, three of them come up; in Tote Placepots, five of them come up; in forecasts, one comes first and the other comes third; in each-way bets, yours finishes fourth, unless it's a sixteen-runner handicap, in which case it finishes fifth.) The last one was Stubbs II, favourite for the novice chase at Cheltenham. A newcomer made ground on him at the second last, almost came down, blundered again at the last, but still got up to win by a head. The horse was a point-to-pointer called The Dikler. Willie Robinson was on board.

The following Thursday, I did another yankee. Three of them came up. The fourth was Well To Do, later famous for winning the Grand National but at that time a nothing-special hurdler with Tim Forster, six years old and 100–8 in a handicap hurdle at Kempton. A stride from the line, Graham Thorner had him in front; but on the line, Willie Robinson had Pantaraxia in front. Willie, why did you do that? Never no yankee no more, no more, never no yankee no more. Bless you, Willie.

It wasn't a good week. The following day I backed Pinehurst Park in the Ascot Valley Gardens Handicap Hurdle. John Jenkins rode him to a comfortable victory, at 13–2, and I started to make arrangements for a small celebration. It was premature, because the race was declared void. Pinehurst Park had won fair and square but Alec Marsh, the Jockey Club's senior starter, had sent them off three minutes early.

I wasn't a very good loser in those days. I'd moan about photo-finish defeats and all the other mishaps that go with betting on horses. The ones I almost backed, but didn't; the ones I almost didn't back, but did; the ones that fell at the last fence, or the first fence, or on the way to the start. I'm much better now; but then, as Dorothy Paget put it, 'I should be. I've had enough practice.'

I caught the tail-end of Arkle's glories but my first real race-horse hero was Persian War, who won three successive Champion Hurdles, the last two while I was at Cambridge. I watched them on television, wanting Persian War to win with an intense and irrational craving. I prayed that he would jump the next hurdle fast and clean; silently urged him on. We knew he would battle, and we loved him for it. He was our champion, and we wanted him to fight off the pretenders. Like Arkle, with Persian War, it wasn't about betting. He was an out-of-the-ordinary horse, with out-of-the-ordinary connections. Henry Alper, who owned him, had a rare talent for being awkward; Jimmy Uttley, who rode him, was a jump jockey who never jumped a fence in his life. Almost alone among his contemporaries, Uttley specialised in riding hurdlers.

In 1968 Persian War set a weight-carrying record when winning the competitive Schweppes Gold Trophy under 11st 13lb, and then broke another when becoming the only horse to win the Triumph Hurdle and Champion Hurdle in successive years. Knowing that the class horse has to give weight to his rivals makes you want him to win. It is what justice demands.

Two years later, Persian War matched Hatton's Grace and Sir Ken by landing the Champion Hurdle for the third time, and he needed to be a great horse to do it. At the start of the season, Persian War had developed breathing problems. A soft palate operation was only partly successful, and he lined up at Cheltenham without a win to his name from five runs. Sentiment as much as reason sent him off the 5–4 favourite. Bobby Moore (the horse, not the footballer) was there as a pacemaker, with Uttley shouting Duncan Hughes on. By the time they reached the fifth hurdle, Persian War had taken it up. They all came at him – Solomon II, Normandy and Escalus, Drumikill, Major Rose and Coral Diver – and Persian War fought them all off. The flood of relief and pleasure.

But not for John Banks, who had laid Persian War to lose £80,000. In 1970, that was a fortune.

When Jeff and Ian and I went racing, we looked out for Banks, because we had read so much about him in the *Sporting Life*. During the late 1960s and early 1970s his name was constantly in the news, and Banks, a bookmaker with a matchless flair for publicity, was a master at getting it there. On the racecourse, he would knock a favourite out from 11–8 on to 11–10 against, watch the other bookmakers follow suit, and then close his own book and wander round backing the horse himself. He liked to remark, 'The odds against winning consistently are 10,000 to 1. I am the one.' It was Banks who made the memorable claim that betting shops were 'a licence to print money.' Not all bookmakers liked him, but the punters loved him, not least because he mocked Ladbrokes. When Weatherbys refused to allow Banks to name a horse Greenwich Mean Stein, after Ladbrokes' boss Cyril Stein, Banks called it Adorable Cyril instead.

Robin Hood handed out ice-creams and balloons, and rosettes declaring, 'I Back with Banks'. 'Where is he today?' asked Banks' advertisements in the *Sporting Life*. On 13 August 1970 he was in the Glasgow Sheriff's Court on charges of speeding and reckless driving. The verdict was 'not proven'. 'Well,' said Banks, hurrying from the hearing, 'that was the Sheriff's opinion, now get on Bookie's Opinion.' Bookie's Opinion conveniently obliged at Catterick that afternoon, and Banks went home allegedly £10,000 richer.

A couple of months later, Jeff and I hitched a lift from Cambridge to the A1. Then we got stuck. We stood with our thumbs in the air and, when nobody stopped, we started to worry about missing the first race. The awful fear of missing the first loomed large in our lives. Later, when there was a car, Ian Carnaby used to leap out and sprint the last half-mile to Stratford or Folkestone, to make sure we lost our money before we arrived. But that day on the A1, nobody stopped. Eventually, we walked up to a lorry which was parked in a lay-by. 'Would you give us a lift?' I asked.

The driver stared down from his cab. 'Do I have to?' he said.

He did, and drove us on through the crisp, clean, blue-skied day, on our way to Leicester. It's wonderful to be on your way to where you want to be going; the expectation.

Three miles from the racecourse we drove into a large room full of fog. Leicester racecourse was in the middle of the room and, at two o'clock, racing was abandoned. Jeff comforted himself with the thought that the racecard might have rarity value and I comforted myself with a cup of tea and a sausage roll. Racecourse catering was one of the few certainties in life, along with the knowledge that there would be nine non-triers during the afternoon, six of them in the seller, none of them spotted by the stewards. As the sausage roll was served, I said what I always used to say: 'Well, it was all right last week.' After that, things didn't seem so bad. We sat down in a room half-empty with people who looked as if they were enjoying hard times, and complained. We complained about the fog and about the sausage rolls, and then went home. I can't remember how.

When we got home, we started thinking about the next day's racing. The next day started when the newspaper shop which opened earliest opened. I arrived on my bicycle, collected the *Sporting Life*, and cycled back to read it over a six o'clock breakfast. I had become familiar with the *Sporting Life* – where things were, how they were laid out. Usually, the first thing I did was turn to the day's cards, and then plod my way through the form; but on 3 October 1970 Jeffrey Bernard's first column appeared in the *Life*.

I can still remember the new joy of sitting in my room in Cambridge early in the morning, the gas fire on, toast in the toaster, reading Bernard's articles. Sometimes I even read them before I looked at the card. In 1970, he was a revelation. Not all his pieces were good, and some were repetitious, but he wrote about racing like nobody else ever had: irreverently, as a punter. He wrote about the things he liked: women, gambling, drinking, Doug Marks, the Irish and Caroline Balding; and the things he didn't like: trainers who took themselves too seriously, British Rail, racecourse catering and people who misspelt his name.

If he wrote now what he wrote then, his in-tray would be swamped with outrage. Bernard's column managed to include a picture of a topless model and a photocopy of a bet struck with a Brighton bookmaker that the winner of the Miss World contest would have a chest measuring 36 inches. She did, at 5–2 against. Taffy Salaman challenged Bernard to a fight for insulting apprentices, and a taxi driver challenged him to another for insulting taxi drivers. If all else failed, and it sometimes did, Bernard had a large bag full of abusive letters to fall back on.

A few years later, when alcohol levels got between Bernard and his cult 'Low Life' column in the *Spectator*, a brief note began to appear, informing readers 'Jeffrey Bernard is unwell.' The *Sporting Life* was the first with the news, although in those days Bernard was 'ill'. It was only later that he became unwell.

On Saturday 3 April 1971 I was on a train to Egham, sitting opposite an old man in a Chelsea pensioner's uniform. Eventually I asked him about his uniform, which is what you have to do when faced by a Chelsea pensioner. He looked very pleased to have been asked, ignored my question, and came up with one of his own: 'Do you know Jimmy Hill?'

'Not personally,' I replied, 'but I've seen his chin.'

'I'm his father.'

I was surprised, but he had ignored my question, so I ignored his answer. 'Have you had a bet on the National?' I asked.

'Yes,' he said. 'Jimmy's tipped me one. I've had a bit on Specify.' Jimmy Hill's father looked proud and I looked patronising, and forget about him until the evening, when I found a betting slip in my pocket. As I rolled it up, to see if I could at least get it into the waste-paper bin first throw, I thought of him, and of Specify, who had won at 28–1.

The following year I didn't see Jimmy Hill's father, but I still took an interest in the National, just as I had done every year since 1967, the year of Foinavon. It was Foinavon who first gave me the idea that you could make money by backing horses who ran more slowly than all the others. Twenty-five years later, I realised I had been mistaken.

In those days, National horses all looked pretty much the same to me: small, perhaps two inches high, a greyish colour, with a touch of television interference across the withers. I didn't actually back Foinavon, or Red Alligator, or Highland Wedding. In 1970 I almost backed Gay Trip, but didn't. Then I had a bad run, during which I didn't back Specify, Well To Do, Red Rum (twice), L'Escargot, Rag Trade, Red Rum (again), Lucius or Rubstic. I think of it as a period when I was gaining experience.

When I got back from Egham, I stopped thinking about the Grand National and started thinking about the Two Thousand Guineas instead. It was billed as a match between Mill Reef and My Swallow. In the betting shop in King Street, there was only one question (apart from what was going to win the next at Catterick): could the good little one (Mill Reef) beat the good big one (My Swallow)? Jeff Connor and I went to Newmarket to find out but, while watchers glanced from the good little one to the good big one and back again, Brigadier Gerard swept imperiously past them both and rendered the question irrelevant.

That autumn I graduated from Cambridge and, in the end,

decided to stick with academia for a while and do research. The students I mixed with spent a lot of time demonstrating and arguing the finer points of socialist doctrine. I couldn't join them on the barricades, because demonstrations invariably clashed with racing, but I shared their dismissiveness of people who showed an interest in making money or exercising power. Within our circle, research was one of the few respectable occupations. I wanted to work somewhere totally different from Cambridge, where a don would sometimes call you into his room merely in order to tell you how clever you both were. There wasn't anywhere much more different than Bradford, and it was here I ended up, thanks to the encouragement of Derek Fraser, a social historian at Bradford University and an inspirational figure: academically brilliant, enthusiastic, full of ideas. The Social Science Research Council funded me for three years' full-time research towards a doctorate, and I embarked on my postgraduate routine, spending the mornings studying the treatment of poverty in the nineteenth century and the afternoons learning how to achieve it in the twentieth.

To begin with, I shared a house with some other research students; then, early in 1972, my wife and I bought a terraced house in Waverley Terrace, off the Great Horton Road. It cost £1,700, had three bedrooms and didn't need a thing doing to it. We had a mortgage of £14 a month. Houses in Bradford were ridiculously cheap, and there were rows of For Sale signs in the roads around Waverley Terrace. 'Why are so many houses for sale?', I naïvely asked one of the sellers. 'Well, luv,' she said, 'They're movin' in, aren't they?' When I looked puzzled, she carried on, 'You know, the Asians.'

Mr and Mrs Petty, who were getting on, lived one door up from us. Gladys lived life through plates of scones. 'What was the outing like, Gladys?'

'Oooh, luv, we had a luvly tea. You should 'ave seen those scones. And there was jam on them, well, it was this thick.'

# Sausage Rolls and Obituaries

Nowadays, I like reading the obituaries in newspapers. It's a good way of catching up on people's news and enables me to enjoy the misfortunes of others. It's a habit I picked up from Gladys, who was an avid reader of the births, marriages and deaths column in the *Bradford Telegraph and Argus*, especially the deaths. Now and again, she would let out a loud shriek and a triumphant, 'Margaret Butterworth's gone!' Outliving all the people you never really liked anyway is one of the last pleasures of old age, a final outburst of man's, and woman's, competitive spirit.

Norman sat quietly, studying the football pools and throwing in the odd wry comment, while Gladys ploughed on. 'Yorkshire born and Yorkshire bred,' she'd often say, 'strong in t'arm and weak in t'ed.' And then she'd laugh a great, screaming laugh. I liked talking to Norman, but one night he started to cough, and just couldn't stop. He coughed so much that in the end he had a heart attack, and died. I missed him.

On the other side were the Kaurs. They came from a small village in Pakistan. Mrs Kaur was young and tiny, with three young children, Baljit, Daljit and Gurjit. She often looked sad, which wasn't surprising, because Mr Kaur was old enough to be her grandfather, but was her husband instead. During the day, Mrs Kaur would sit at the back door which faced into the yard behind, and pound spices in a bowl: thud, thud, thud. During the night, the bathroom door would bang and Mr Kaur would cough a loud retching cough, the legacy of tuberculosis. Then he would cough another one. One summer the Kaurs made a trip to Pakistan, and Mr Kaur didn't come back; he died on the flight. Relatives hurried and scurried in and out of the house, and very soon the sad expression disappeared from Mrs Kaur's face.

While my wife gained affection by her ability to say, 'Good morning, how are you?' in Urdu, I became a junior member at Wetherby. One bus to Leeds, another to Wetherby, and then a walk over the bridge across the A1 to the corner of the course, and diagonally across it. Wetherby was a good, fair course, a true test of jumping. I remember the mighty Supermaster winning his fifth race in a row under 12st 12lb, and Frankie Howerd laughing away in the winner's enclosure. I remember the stable lass crying when Tembo was sold out of David Barron's yard after winning the seller; and, the day after, an emotional double for the wheelchair-bound Cliff Boothman, when Camus won at 50–1 and Valairon did the same at 6–1. The anticipation of going to Wetherby was something felt for days beforehand: studying the entries, wondering what would run, keeping an eye on the weather, not wanting anything to come between me and being there. Arranging things to make sure.

One week every year, Ian Carnaby and Jeff Connor and I used to go for a racing holiday, to Yarmouth or Warwick, Folkestone, Newcastle or Leicester. I looked forward to it with a wanting that I can't imagine today. We usually set off broke, and came back broker. But most days I walked down the hill to Bradford Central Library for opening time, got the lift up to the archives section on the top floor, sat down with my fountain pen, filled with Quink (Royal Blue), and an A4 (narrow-lined) pad, and worked my way steadily through the pages of the Bradford Board of Guardians' minute books and the *Bradford Observer*.

It wasn't always Bradford Central Library, nor always the *Bradford Observer*. Sometimes it was Leeds University Library, or the social services offices in Keighley; the West Riding registry of deeds at Wakefield or, for a lengthy spell, the British Library and the Public Record Office in London. Mountains of correspondence between the central and local authorities; huge numbers of parliamentary reports and returns; decades of newspapers and minute books, rate books and workhouse books, pamphlets and posters, articles and theses. I still have the box files full of notes and card indexes full of cards.

In those days I had a voracious appetite for work. I worked morning, noon and night, Saturdays and Sundays – except in the afternoons. If I was working in Bradford, about an hour before the first race I'd stroll down to a café a few doors away from Ladbrokes on Hall Ings, and settle down for a second look at the *Sporting Life*, with a prawn roll and a cup of tea. Then, eager and content, I moved on to the betting shop. Inside the door, on the right, was a black-covered bench, where I used to sit. At the far end was a tramp who had married a lettuce and pickle roll. They lived together in uneasy harmony. I liked to arrive well before the first race, to be sure of hearing news of any non-runners, or jockey changes, or overweights, and the state of the going. You couldn't always trust the boardman to put those things up on the board.

Sometimes I sat next to an older man with a posh voice. One day I noticed that none of his betting slips had a till receipt stamped on them. He would get up and walk over to the 'Bet Here' counter, but when he came back his slip had no receipt on it. I didn't ask him about it. I thought, perhaps he has no money; he has no money but wants to seem to be a player; maybe it embarrasses him. Then I noticed the way he talked to young men in the shop, and when he asked me if I'd like to join him for a bottle of wine at his home, I fled to the Mecca shop up Great Horton Road. I was safe there, and respected. I know that because, on 18 January 1975, when I asked for £4 on Ben More at 10–1 for the Wills Premier Chase Final at Haydock, the manager rang regional headquarters to clear it and then told me I could have 6–1.

## Chapter Three

# Heroic Eccentrics

I have never seen a horse jump the Grand National fences as Crisp jumped them in 1973. Magnificent, near-black, way out in front. One majestic leap after another until you were gripped, hanging nervously on the next fence. The boldness and power and courage – and, in the end, the cruelty of sudden, desperate tiredness. Carrying 12st. Rolling, all gone, and the awful sight of Red Rum, whom we had not yet learned to love, closing remorselessly, carrying 10st 5lb.

That is what you must not forget: 12st; 10st 5lb. It is a big difference, and that is why, for me and many others, Crisp's performance was the best ever seen in the National.

At that time, most horses, trainers and jockeys were just names on the racing page, pieces of the form jigsaw, words in a commentary. I had never met any of them, but I got to know the personalities, a little, from a distance. Crisp was an exception, because it wasn't usually the best horses or the most successful trainers who attracted my interest, but small-time performers I came to know from poring over the humblest of races. The media often make the mistake of assuming that the most successful are the most interesting. The most interesting are those who have known success, but have had to cope with failure.

There was satisfaction in mastering the minutiae of poor law administration, and there was a similar satisfaction in getting to know something, but not enough, about the ways of men like Lieutenant-Colonel 'Ricky' Vallance, Peter Poston and Richmond Sturdy. Later, I made pilgrimages to see Vallance, who was dead, and Poston, who – for a while – was alive. I never did get to visit Sturdy, dead or alive.

Research skills are useful in tracking people down, and I managed to find Kenny Rivers, who had once been a conditional jockey at Vallance's yard in Bishops Cannings, in Wiltshire, and 'Titch' Fowler, the former head lad. Bishops Cannings is one of those small English villages where the church would still seem optimistically large even if every inhabitant prayed regularly for a winner. The pub, The Crown, stands next to the church, offering its time-honoured reward for listening to the vicar's sermons; and behind the churchyard stands Lynes House, the largest in the village. Here Vallance had lived; but by the time I visited, the stable block had been converted into houses. Someone was sleeping in the box where Sea Pigeon had briefly been isolated with ringworm; someone else was sitting down to eat breakfast on the spot where Red Candle, the winner of the 1972 Mackeson Gold Cup and 1973 Hennessy, had once stood up to eat his.

Fowler told me that, in those days, Lieutenant-Colonel 'Ricky' Vallance used to step out in his underpants and slippers at a frosty six o'clock in the morning and wash his hair in a tank of rainwater. Later, he might dip his nine Maltese terriers in a washing machine and confront Mrs Vallance with some extracts from the *Oxford Dictionary of Slang*. The Colonel's wife kept show ponies, and Vallance couldn't stand the sight of them. The head lad remembered one marital Somme which started with an oil-filled radiator flying out of a bedroom window and ended, as they always did, with Vallance bellowing the word 'darling'.

In 1971 David Elsworth, who later earned fame as the trainer of Desert Orchid, turned up at the yard with a couple of horses. The arrangement was that Vallance would train them and Elsworth ride out; but the newcomer found himself doing the training too. Red Candle's success in the Mackeson and Hennessy should have given Elsworth a step up the training ladder but, six months after the Hennessy, it all went wrong. In April 1974, Kenny Rivers rode a horse called Well Briefed at Wincanton. He was unplaced. Early in May, at Fontwell, Johnny Haine took over. Haine was a wonderfully stylish rider, but he had been warned off in 1968 after an enquiry into the running of Calling Sonny had concluded that Haine 'deliberately made no effort to win the race'. At Fontwell, Well Briefed was unplaced again but, nine days later, heavily backed, the same partnership won the twenty-runner Tiverton Handicap Hurdle at Devon and Exeter by six lengths. The stewards refused to accept Elsworth's and Vallance's explanations for the apparent improvement in form, and Vallance was disqualified for a year.

The decision rankled with Elsworth, who had to fight his way back into training via market trading and a livery yard. 'It cost me four years,' he told me. 'I'm not bitter; it's a long time ago, but the relevant point has never been aired. They said the horse must have been stopped on its previous outing. It's a mystery to me how we succeeded in stopping the horse, *if* we did, without involving the jockey. Yet we must have done it without his cooperation because Johnny Haine was exonerated.' The stewards worked in peculiar ways in those days, their duties to misperform.

Vallance went on to lose his trainer's licence once more and his driver's licence twice more; but the more licences he lost, the better the locals loved him. When the evenings were over, they pulled the Colonel out of the ditches or, on one famous occasion, out of a recently dug grave in the churchyard, and pushed him on to Saxon Warrior, who was tethered outside the pub and knew his way home. When Vallance died, he left Kenny Rivers £1,000 to make up for the times when he'd overlooked paying him. Now, if you call in at The Crown or The Bridge Inn, and mention the Colonel's name, they will all smile and say that he was well loved.

When I visited Peter Poston, in 1989, it was ten years since he had given up training. I found him sitting in a tiny caravan which was sitting in somebody's front garden in Newmarket; an impish figure, with the face of a child. He was working as a jockey's agent for Allan Mackay. It was a difficult job, because at that time Mackay was in police custody being questioned about drug smuggling.

Poston had a theory about breeding. If you went back far enough (about 300 years), every racehorse traced back to the Godolphin Arabian or the Byerley Turk or the Darley Arabian. That meant they all had the same breeding, more or less. What was the point of paying a lot of money for a racehorse when you could get virtually the same horse for almost nothing? In 1961 Poston put his theory to the test by buying a yearling filly called Athene for 140 guineas. She didn't win a race as a two-year-old, so Poston gave her away as a prize in a £1 raffle. It was a very generous gesture, because Athene later had a son called Rheingold, who finished second in the 1972 Derby and in 1973 won the Prix de l'Arc de Triomphe.

Homefield cost Poston a bit more: 150 guineas. By the middle of June 1973, the five-year-old had managed to run twenty-five times without winning. Then, to everyone's amazement, he suddenly won five of his next seven starts, including the Tennent Trophy at Ayr. Homefield fell back exhausted, had a season off, followed it up with twenty-one successive defeats, and then, as an eight-year-old, won another five from seven.

All Homefield's wins were gained with apprentices on board and most of them involved a long journey from Poston's New-market yard. If you suffered from travel sickness, working for Poston was likely to kill you. This wanderlust might have had something to do with the fact that during the 1970s the Levy Board handed out travel allowances. Poston didn't train many winners, but he had an awful lot of runners in Scotland, and it intrigued me. I'm glad I visited him when I did, because two years later he was dead.

Richmond Chartres Sturdy had already died by then, leaving a son and four daughters with names as exotic as his own: Arabella, Atalanta, Marine and Candida. I never spoke to Sturdy, but I'd sometimes see him, usually at Salisbury. It's one of my favourite racecourses, and not only because, one day in 1976, the one-eyed Striker cruised home in the Danebury Selling Stakes. The countryside is beautiful and the sun always seems to be shining. If there's time, I call in at The Victoria and Albert in Netherhampton, a mile from the course. It's nice there. You should do the same. When I reach the racecourse, I walk up to the top of the stand, where the house martins live, and look across to Salisbury Cathedral.

In the old days I'd often see a thin, shambling figure, standing near the Tote windows, working out his dual forecasts. You could always spot Sturdy, because his shoes looked as if they had been his great-grandfather's only pair. The further up his body you moved, the stranger he became, until you reached his head. Inside it, the Wiltshire trainer was plotting a complicated coup; or that's what he liked to think. He would sit in the local betting shop surrounded by form books and work out how he was going to empty the bookmakers' satchels.

Sturdy didn't stop his horses, he just ran them over the wrong trip or when they weren't fit. He knew they weren't fit, because they'd been kept standing in their boxes twiddling their hooves for a few days. When he finally let them out on to the gallops, they went crazy. John Reid, who was an apprentice at the time, once set off with three others and was the only one to come back.

It was difficult to know exactly how Sturdy's mind worked. In 1974 he ran Grand Orient and Barbarie Corsaire in the Derby, although neither had the remotest chance of finishing within sight of the winner. The two 200–1 shots had both warmed up for Epsom by getting thrashed in maiden races, and Sturdy probably ran both of them to make sure that at least one didn't finish last (one of them didn't). Perhaps it was part of an elaborate plot, which reached its climax a month later when Barbarie Corsaire, with Reid on board, won the Rutherglen Maiden Plate at Hamilton; or two years later, when Grand Orient finally broke his duck at Beverley.

The year after Sturdy's Derby, he laid out a modest hurdler called No Camping for a selling race at Southwell. David Elsworth was Sturdy's assistant at the time, and when the great day arrived, Elsworth and jockey Colin Brown arrived with it. When they got to the yard, Sturdy couldn't be roused.

'I don't feel like going,' he shouted down the stairs. 'You go.'

This proved difficult, since No Camping was coughing and Sturdy had forgotten to hire a horsebox. But Elsworth is a determined man, and he had an idea. An hour later, No Camping was loaded into the back of a baker's van. Brown sat in the driver's seat and Sturdy, grumpy but out of bed, sat in the middle. For forty minutes, nothing was said. Then Sturdy spoke. 'I don't think it'll win, anyway.' But No Camping did win; just.

I miss following Richmond Chartres Sturdy, and I miss watching Knockroe. Most of the unending stream of horses who passed through my head were run-of-the-mill performers, though I found them totally engaging. There was an intellectual appeal in gathering and analysing information about

horses – their characteristics, their style, their racing requirements – whatever the limits of their abilities. Races were a
never-ending procession of crossword puzzles. The majority of
big-race winners passed me by, because I was immersed in
selling races and lowly handicaps, races confined to lady riders
and apprentices. Now and again, though, a good-class horse
would stir me; and once, just once, there was a horse called
Knockroe.

When I started to write about racing, he was the horse I most
wanted to write about. So I contacted his owner, the late Major
Victor McCalmont, and Knockroe's trainers, Major Peter
Nelson and his son John, and some of the jockeys who had
ridden my favourite horse.

'I'll never have one like him again,' McCalmont told me. 'He
was a once in a lifetime. If he had been an entire and eligible to
run, he would have won eight Derbys out of ten.'

Wishful thinking? Not according to Peter Nelson, who rated
Knockroe more highly than Snow Knight, his 1974 Derby
winner. 'Snow Knight was a good, genuine horse,' said Nelson,
'but Knockroe was better. He had supreme natural ability. If he
had given his all, he would have been unbeatable, but the horse
had a peculiar temperament.'

That is one way of putting it. McCalmont was less polite.

'Knockroe was always a bastard. When he had his injections
as a foal, he was like a bomb. We had him with his bum stuck
out of the door of the loose box. The vet had to run past and jab
the needle in him as he went by, the next time the syringe, and
the next time press it. He was quite impossible. People were
always telling me how intelligent he was but he wasn't, he was
a bloody fool.'

Training him was a unique experience. 'At home,' Nelson
recalled, 'he was unpredictable. You had to make special
arrangements for him, but you could never find the key.

'Sometimes we'd drive the car up to the gallops, bang on the roof and give a toot to set him off, and then he'd work upsides the car. He had great natural speed. We clocked him at 44mph up a severe incline. Not bad for a stayer!'

As a three-year-old Knockroe was galloped over six furlongs at level weights with Apollo Nine, who won that year's Stewards' Cup carrying 9st 5lb. Knockroe beat his galloping companion out of sight. When he put his eccentric mind to it, he could beat almost anything. Unraced at two, in 1971 Knockroe won five of his ten outings, including the Group Three Cumberland Lodge Stakes at Ascot. For his final run that season, Knockroe travelled to Longchamp for the Prix du Conseil Municipal. The stalls handlers took exception to Knockroe's awkward behaviour, he took exception to their vigorous response and that, McCalmont suspected, was 'the beginning of his impossibility. He never forgave the human race.'

Even so, Knockroe had a tremendous season as a four-year-old. It wasn't just that he won four Group races – the Jockey Club Stakes, Yorkshire Cup, Cumberland Lodge Stakes and St Simon stakes – it was the way he did it. The way he did it was one of the reasons why I liked him so much. Knockroe liked to come wide and from behind, way behind. He came late and fast, very fast. There was an anticipation about watching Knockroe that few other horses have ever generated. On his day, you could spot the moment when the decision, and it was Knockroe's decision alone, hung in the balance. Would he say 'yes', would he go? If he did, he'd use a scything turn of foot to cut down the opposition and take the breath away, for when Knockroe was good, he was very good, even though, when he was bad, he was bloody awful.

When Eric Eldin took over from Lester Piggott for Knockroe's last race as a four-year-old, in the St Simon Stakes, he experienced the quirky grey at his knife-edge best.

'If you moved a muscle,' Eldin recalled, 'he wouldn't go. To try and lay up was hopeless, and you didn't wait with him, he waited with you.'

In the St Simon, Knockroe kept Eldin waiting and waiting until, finally, when all seemed lost, patience was rewarded. With less than two furlongs to go, Knockroe decided to join the race; within a furlong, he had reached the front; between there and the post, lost interest as quickly as he had found it, and hung on by a short head from Sol'Argent.

But in the Princess of Wales's Stakes Knockroe refused to race at all; and the infuriating grey opened his five-year-old season by being beaten five lengths by Rheingold in the John Porter Stakes after giving the 1972 Derby runner-up 4lb and literally half a furlong start. Worse was to come. On his next three outings, Knockroe declined to take any active part. At Kempton, Frankie Durr lost patience with him and experimented with the whip. It was a mistake. Roughly one second after Durr's experiment started, the jockey and the horse were thirty yards apart. Lester Piggott had already deserted Knockroe, and so had all sane punters, but Nelson persuaded McCalmont to risk just one more humiliation, in the valuable Weetabix Wildlife Handicap at Epsom. Perhaps a course as eccentric as the horse might provoke Knockroe's interest.

It was two days after Morston had won the Derby. McCalmont dug himself into the bar, to prepare for another indignity, while the starter invited Eldin to make an early attempt on the stalls. Eldin held back and, when Knockroe followed the others behind, he felt that everything was going to be all right.

'He didn't tail himself off, although he was with those at the tail. I took him to the outside, to race on his own, and he came through and won on the bridle. It couldn't have been easier.' Or quicker. Since Mahmoud's victory in the 1936 Derby, there had been countless attempts on his course record. Nearly forty years later, in 1973, it was Knockroe who broke it, easing down. His wayward talent covered the Derby course more than

45

two seconds faster than Morston.

After the race, there was a scene that stuck in the trainer's memory. 'The vet came up to me,' Nelson remembered, 'and said, "I'm sorry, Major Nelson, but I'm going to have to check your horse again." He couldn't believe Knockroe's heartbeat could be so slow. I knew the reason, though. Knockroe hadn't really exerted himself.'

At Brighton, another switchback track, Knockroe won again under 10st 4lb, but was injured in the process and went back to McCalmont's farm in Ireland. Connections had a brief stab at turning him into a hurdler but, as McCalmont put it, 'We never got him inside the wings.' Having recruited a jockey with a stunted instinct for self-preservation, a tempting life insurance policy and a pressing desire to test the theory of life after death, he then unleashed Knockroe into the hunting field. It is not unusual for a horse to terrify its rider, but it takes a Knockroe to terrify an entire hunt.

'Hunting was fun for him,' McCalmont remembered, 'but not for anyone else. He spent most of the time up on his hind legs or attacking the person on the horse in front.' After two tries, they decided to give the hat-trick a miss.

In 1976 the ageing rogue put in an appearance at Limerick and then returned to Nelson's yard, now in the hands of his son John. When Knockroe arrived, he was still wearing heavy hunting shoes, because the farrier in Ireland hadn't been able to get near him to take them off. A couple of unpromising runs later, Knockroe was retired to McCalmont's stud where he died from a heart attack, or possibly a brain tumour. That would certainly explain a lot.

There really never will be another Knockroe. There will probably be other Amrullahs though, and maybe the occasional Broxadella and Not Too Far. There's something perversely appealing about horses like them, unless you have to ride them.

A lifetime of not trying made Amrullah a minor cult figure in jump racing. When he finally retired, in 1992, he had spent eight and a half years and seventy-four races perfecting the art of not winning. It wasn't that he couldn't win; it was just that he didn't want to. He wasn't unreasonable about it. He was prepared to finish in front of good horses, like Floyd and Hypnosis, as long as there was still another horse in front of him.

Terry Thorn was Amrullah's greatest fan, which was lucky for Amrullah, because Thorn owned him. 'I always back him to win,' Thorn told me. 'I walk down the rails and shout, "Who'll give me 100–1?" I don't have to wait long.

'I was once offered £40,000 for Amrullah but I thought that if someone was prepared to pay that much for him, he must be worth having, so I kept him. I suppose it was a mistake.

'I know he stops dead if you touch him with a whip,' he acknowledged, 'but he doesn't object to everything. He likes biting and kicking. I'd ride him out myself, but John Bridger won't let me. He says that Amrullah's already put three people in hospital. When he broke Jill Bridger's arm, John said to me, "Don't worry, Terry, it was a lovely clean break." '

That's the sort of horse he was – a bit like Broxadella, only less dangerous. Having finished last of fourteen on her only outing as a two-year-old, Arthur Jones's filly began to behave strangely at the start. At first it was nothing too serious: a violent swerve to the left, the occasional refusal to race, the depositing of the unwelcome jockey on the unyielding turf. Then things got out of hand. In 1984, at Pontefract, Broxadella shot out of stall 13, whipped round and shot back into stall 11. After that, the Jockey Club wouldn't let her race on the Flat, so Mark Brisbourne took on the responsibility for racing her over hurdles.

Broxadella was fine until she started to get fit. Then she threw away her brakes and engaged top speed. If you tried to tell her off, she'd lie down on the ground in a rage. Three years after the unpleasantness at Pontefract, Brisbourne pointed Broxadella at Bangor's hurdle course. It took three helpers to get the jockey on board, and then Broxadella tried to lie down. The unhappy pair finally set off, last. By the second hurdle they were twenty lengths clear. Then Broxadella stopped. Brisbourne thought it was time to give somebody else a chance but, when Peter Davis tried her out, Broxadella first refused to race, and then mimicked her Bangor run. At this point they gave up.

Connections of Not Too Far had a similar experience. One day at Warwick, one of my favourite tracks, I was standing in the stands – the ones which feel as if you wouldn't want to be there if they were on fire – when John Carroll asked Jack Berry's two-year-old to make the transition from the parade ring to the racecourse. Not Too Far thought she had gone far enough. First she dug her toes in, and then, when Carroll politely suggested that it was time to be going, she flung herself to the ground. Limping, Carroll remounted. In the ring, bookmakers pushed Not Too Far out further, from 2–1 to 9–2. There weren't many takers. Eventually, against all the odds, Not Too Far arrived at the stalls and was goaded into them. In that mood, there was no way she could possibly win the Man Appeal Selling Stakes. But she did, by a neck, having battled gamely all the way up the straight. All the same, and wisely, they didn't race her again.

At least she hadn't cost much, in a world populated by people with more money than sense. Businessmen's brains rarely survive contact with racing stables; it is like introducing a blow-lamp to a jelly. Take Heyshott – Clive Holmes did, for 38,000 guineas. Granted, this was a lot less than the $575,000 Heyshott had cost Khaled Abdulla as a yearling, and Guy Harwood had trained the well-bred colt to win his first two races. That was the good news. The bad news was that

Heyshott refused to race on his next two outings and, when Harwood gave him one more shot, armed with blinkers, he started, but barely finished. Timeform awarded him the rare notoriety of a double squiggle, denoting 'an arrant rogue or thorough jade', and warned that he 'must be left alone'.

Mr Holmes, a wealthy owner and amateur rider turned trainer, begged to differ. When I asked him why, he replied, 'Because Heyshott had a lot of ability, but seemed to have a problem with the starting stalls. There are no stalls in hurdle races, so we could have had a top-class hurdler on our hands.' It was a bold move, but horses like Heyshott don't need stalls to destroy their appetite for racing. A month after buying his exciting prospect, Holmes unveiled Heyshott at Sandown Park, where he was pulled up. Four months later, he turned up in the Victor Ludorum Hurdle at Haydock, and finished last of the ten finishers.

When John White, Holmes's talented assistant, set up on his own, he took Heyshott with him, but it didn't make any difference. After finishing a distant fourth of five in a novice hurdle at Plumpton, Heyshott refused to race on the Flat at Warwick, and very nearly did the same at Stratford, eventually completing the course last of fifteen finishers. A year later, in December 1989, Heyshott was given a final chance, on Lingfield's all-weather hurdle course. Six finished, and he was the last of them, beaten 101 lengths.

In the days when I used to read Timeform's *Racehorses* annual from beginning to end, Abalvina to Zyppon, I liked to keep an eye out for the follies of the over-rich. There were plenty to choose from, including Fusion, who was bought for 600,000 guineas as a yearling, gelded ominously early, and failed to finish nearer than fourth in his first five races. When Imperial Brush (10,500 guineas) thrashed him at Salisbury, Khaled Abdulla decided the time had come to admit defeat. Barney Curley took Fusion off his hands for 15,000 guineas, but it was Robert Earnshaw who finally got a race out of him, a seller at Lingfield.

There's something heartwarming about that, and about Snaafi Dancer, the best-known folly of all, bought by Sheikh Mohammed for over $10 million in 1983, but too slow to be allowed into a horsebox. Ken Carey, one of John Dunlop's long-serving lads, told me that he once rode Snaafi Dancer on the gallops. 'I couldn't believe how slow he was.' He wasn't much good at anything else, either. Twelve years on, the *News of the World* caught up with Snaafi Dancer, a pet on a farm in Connecticut. There was a picture of a horse with a bubble coming out of its mouth. 'I can't run . . . I can't race . . . and I can't even bonk.'

# Chapter Four

## A Boardman's Life

The *Bradford Telegraph and Argus* ran a weekly racing competition, with a prize of a day at the races and a free £4 bet. In May 1974 I won it, and on my prize outing to the next Saturday meeting at Thirsk I put my £4 on Carew Lady, a 4–1 shot in the seller. Dave Thom's filly was beaten four lengths by Carne Gray but was awarded the race on an objection. Then I backed Ye-Yo in the ladies' race, partly because Pat Rohan's four-year-old was ridden by Diana Bissill, one of the best lady riders around: and it won, at 14–1.

Ladies' races were the nearest I ever came to making it pay. Most punters wouldn't touch ladies' races with someone else's bargepole and, if one was on television, one or other of the pundits invariably trotted out the phrase, 'this isn't a race to bet on.' How wrong they were. There were none better.

The first ladies' race was run at Kempton in 1972. In the early races, the field was strung out after a furlong. Some riders were run away with, others kicked on at a suicidal pace, while negotiating a bend utterly defeated many of the rest. The conclusion punters drew from all this was that ladies' races were a lottery, a joke, fit to appear only on a lunatic's betting slip. Their only value was novelty value, and that is how the races were seen, patronisingly, as novelty events. In reality they presented a golden opportunity, because in ladies' and amateur riders' races there was a huge gulf between the best riders and the worst, far greater than in any professional race. The top professional jockeys rarely returned a profit to a level stake; the top amateurs rarely failed to. The niceties of handicapping, of X being 6lb better off with Y for a length, counted for nothing if Y had one of the best lady riders on board and X didn't. Many amateurs were incapable of getting anything like the best out of their mounts. You had to change the way you looked at a race.

But first you had to discover who was good, and who wasn't. Unless you worked on the racecourse, that was a much more difficult task than it is today. There was no SIS, and few amateur races were televised. Unless you were prepared to judge by the raw results, you had to be there. I often went racing purely to see how a particular lady rider rode, and it was the best information available. I liked Brooke Sanders, Jenny Goulding, and Diana Bissill, but the best was Elain Mellor. Compared to most of her rivals, Mellor was in a class of her own, and it wasn't long before Sir Mark Prescott, one of the shrewdest of trainers, started to exploit the fact. Prescott and Mellor teamed up to win the prestigious Ladies' Diamond Stakes at Ascot two years in a row with Mandalus, in 1977 and 1978, and Mellor was lady champion eight times.

Following Mellor was the best betting step I ever took, but it was Diana Bissill who provided me with one of my most satisfying wins. At the Newmarket Autumn Sales in 1974, a decent three-year-old colt called Irish Harmony was sold out of Doug Smith's yard for 7,400 guineas, a fair sum in those days. To my fascination, the buyer was Diana Bissill. The horse was sent to Pat Rohan's Malton yard, and I waited and watched for his entries. In May 1975, Irish Harmony finished a well beaten fourth in an amateur riders' handicap at Ayr, carrying 11st 1lb on heavy ground. Two weeks later, he returned to a much drier Ayr for a conditions race, the Brooke Bond Tea Cup Ladies' Race over ten furlongs. It was the right race for him and I put £40 on at 9–4. It doesn't sound much now, but at the time it was three weeks' wages. I remember listening to the commentary in the Ladbrokes shop where I was working. Irish Harmony won by an easy four lengths.

The following year, at Kempton, Bissill won on Irish Harmony again, at 20–1. I was there, but I didn't back him. Pity.

Then, gradually, I started to notice Diana Jones, the daughter of Arthur Jones, whose main claim to fame was having trained Merry Deal to win the 1957 Champion Hurdle. Diana had her first race in 1975, but it was another three years before she rode her first winner; and that was the problem. The horses she rode weren't good enough to win. Most trainers hadn't got a clue about the ability of the various lady riders. They knew who had been riding winners, and that was all. It was some sort of a guide, but it was hard on a rider like Jones, who didn't often win, and wouldn't ring trainers for rides. 'I think if I was good enough,' she told me, 'they'd have noticed me and they'd have rung me up.' But racing is crueller than that. In the days before SIS arrived, you could ride a perfect race, finish sixth and no one would notice.

During the late 1970s and early 1980s, I watched Diana many times, riding horses with no prospect of winning. Usually, she was the one hugging the rails into the straight, sitting off a too-fast pace, perfectly placed if the horse was good enough, more effective in a finish than most lady riders – but the horse rarely was good enough. Typically, Diana thought her best performance was when she got the five-year-old maiden, Calm Ship, into fourth place at Edinburgh in 1978, at

33–1. The same year she finished second on Reparation, a 12–1 shot, in the Ladies' Diamond Stakes at Ascot, for Gavin Hunter. He used Jones sometimes, and so did Ian Balding for a while; and, when Mellor wasn't available, Prescott put Diana up. By 1989, fourteen years after her first ride, she had gathered together a motley collection of over twenty winners, including a few over hurdles.

Some time during the mid-eighties I wrote to Diana and she invited me to visit their yard at Pentre David, near Oswestry. They were wonderfully welcoming: Arthur, a lovely man, Isobel, his bubbly wife, Diana and her sisters, Victoria and Alex. I had never been to a racing stable before. Pentre David was out in the countryside, a border farm, with an open door and a relaxed atmosphere; dogs and people drifted in and out. The Joneses showed me all their horses – most of them 'challenges', like High Port and Prince Reviewer, a five-year-old maiden when Diana won the Ladies' Derby on him at Ripon in 1983. I saw Russian Winter, the stable star, who had won a seller for Pat Haslam on his sixteenth start, failed over hurdles, won a small race at Hamilton for Don Plant, gone in his wind, been led out of the Doncaster sale ring unsold and then won sixteen times for Arthur Jones, including eight races at Ayr, where a race was named after him.

And I began to understand a bit better. Diana was too modest and self-deprecating to feel frustrated at not getting the opportunities to match her ability; didn't want to ring for a ride and risk upsetting another rider; was fearful of pressing her case and then disappointing the trainer who had put his faith in her.

'I'm lucky to have had the chances I've had,' she told me. 'There are times when you wish you were riding one of the good Newmarket horses, but if I ride a horse which has never been placed before, and it gets placed, then I've achieved something.'

There are pleasures beyond winning, small satisfactions and achievements, shared with friends.

'It's not been any good to me financially,' said Arthur, a man who couldn't sound bitter if he tried, 'but it's something you've spent your life at and I would still do the same again, because you meet so many nice people.'

Diana kept plugging away, long after most of her early rivals had retired, and in 1993 she finally won the Lady Amateur Riders' Championship. I felt enormously pleased. Yet it was strange that it should happen then, because the standard of race-riding among amateurs had improved greatly since Diana scored her first win on Wickwell at Doncaster in 1978. Ironically, wider recognition of her ability came at a time when the pool of competent riders was bigger than it had been during years when she had few fancied rides. People notice when you win.

For years, I made a profit betting in amateur riders' races. It's a pity I didn't stick to them. Now, although they still have their attractions, they are a world apart from those early races. The gulf between good riders and bad has narrowed greatly. Today's amateurs take a professional approach, and that has killed the goose with the golden eggs.

In the days when ladies' races were in their infancy, I used to study the form to death. It didn't matter how many race meetings there were, I ploughed through the lot. On August Bank Holiday Monday 1974 there were eleven. As I plodded through the pages of the *Sporting Life*, the newsprint blackening my fingertips, one horse caught my eye – Opera Cloak. It puzzled me; I couldn't understand it. Opera Cloak was trained by Tony Collins, in Scotland, yet he was down to run at Plumpton, in Sussex. Collins only trained a few horses, and rarely had a winner; at this point he hadn't had one for eighteen months. He never, ever, sent horses to racecourses in the south of England. He just didn't do it. And Opera Cloak was a very moderate novice chaser, with no obvious chance of winning the race at Plumpton. What on earth was he doing there?

I checked to see if Collins had any other runners. Ankerwyke was down to run at Southwell, near Nottingham – and that was odd too, because Collins didn't usually have runners at Southwell either. I carried on looking, and finally arrived at Cartmel, on the edge of the Lake District. Collins had entered two horses for the Ulverston Novices' Hurdle, Racionzer and Gay Future. The jockey down to partner Gay Future was an amateur rider called Mr J. McNeill. I had never heard of Mr McNeill, and it appeared to be Gay Future's debut. It didn't look very promising.

I thought about it for a few minutes. There was something. Then I relaxed. Maybe Opera Cloak was moving to a new yard in the south, and was taking in Plumpton on the way. That might be it. I made a mental note to check how Collins' horses got on. They would probably all lose.

But they didn't. When I looked in the *Sporting Life* the next morning, I saw that Gay Future had won, by fifteen lengths, at 10–1; and my curiosity bubbled up again. The winning rider wasn't Mr J. McNeill, but Mr T. A. Jones: Tim Jones, one of Ireland's best amateur riders. Tim Jones had crossed the Irish Sea to ride a horse for Tony Collins in a race worth £204. Opera Cloak and Ankerwyke were both non-runners. That was as close as I got to spotting the most celebrated coup in modern racing.

Gay Future wasn't as inexperienced as readers of the *Sporting Life* and the English form book imagined. In April, he had won an amateur riders' Flat race at Thurles, in Ireland, where he was prepared for the Cartmel race.

The day after Gay Future's victory, bookmakers reported that there had been a flood of £5 and £10 doubles and trebles on Collins' horses: Gay Future and Opera Cloak; Gay Future and Ankerwyke; Gay Future, Opera Cloak and Ankerwyke. Of course, that was clever. For a betting coup to succeed, the right horse has to win, but winning the race is only half the battle; the easy half. The hard part is getting your money on, at the right odds. Even in 1974, bookmakers had a decent alarm system. You couldn't just wander around London, calling in, a stranger, at one betting shop after another, £5 win Gay Future at one shop, £10 win Gay Future in the next. The alarm bells would soon have been ringing, and bookmakers would have taken steps to make sure that Gay Future started at a much shorter price than 10–1, if they agreed to take the bets at all.

The beauty of the Gay Future coup was that bookmakers were lulled into a false sense of security. They thought they were dealing with bets requiring two or three horses to win; but they weren't. In a double, if one of the selections is a non-runner, the stake goes on to the remaining selection. The same applies if two of the three selections in a treble don't run. Only the conspirators knew that Opera Cloak and Ankerwyke would be non-runners, and that all the win doubles and trebles would end up as win singles on Gay Future.

Tony Collins travelled all the way from Scotland to Plumpton to tell the stewards that the horsebox carrying Opera Cloak had broken down.

By the time the bookmakers realised they weren't dealing with multiple bets, but with a battalion of singles, it was too late. Cartmel hadn't been chosen by accident. There was no 'blower' service at the small, picturesque Cumbrian course, and someone was monopolising the telephone kiosk. The bookmakers couldn't shorten Gay Future's starting price by backing him at the racecourse, because they couldn't contact the racecourse. In desperation, Ladbrokes sent a representative by car. He got stuck in the Bank Holiday traffic.

Standing on the railway station at Plumpton, Collins dialled the number of the telephone kiosk at Cartmel. A policeman answered. 'Can you tell me what won the last race?', asked Collins.

The policeman wasn't amused. 'There are 2,000 cars queuing up to leave the course and you want me to find out what won the last?' Collins isn't short of charm, and he used it on the policeman. 'Gay Future,' said the policeman, 'at 10–1.' '10–1?' gasped Collins. 'You've got to be kidding.'

In the betting ring at the racecourse, members of the team had put £400 on Racionzer, Gay Future's stablemate, in order to push the winner's price out.

When the stable lad prepared Gay Future in one of the saddling boxes, he washed him down with soap flakes to make it look as if Gay Future was sweating badly. Jones rounded things off nicely by letting his stirrup leathers down a few holes, after the fashion of a rank amateur, to convince any doubting observers that he was, indeed, a true no-hoper. When he arrived at the start he pulled them up again.

It worked, but bookmakers don't like being caught out, and the Betting Office Licensees Association quickly recommended that its members suspend payment pending a police investigation. The investigation revealed that the brains behind the coup belonged to Tony Murphy, a former part-owner of Gay Future. Eddie O'Grady, a leading Irish trainer, had prepared the horse. Six men had travelled from Ireland, armed with £36,000.

Punters rarely get the bookmakers' trousers down. When they do, other punters don't begrudge them their success, unless it involves a horse not having tried in its previous races. Murphy and his gang were folk heroes. They had done what we all wanted to do. It was said that Collins stood to win about £50,000, and that the coup would have netted a grand total of £250,000, a far bigger fortune then than it sounds now. But they didn't get their money. In March 1975, on the eve of the Cheltenham Festival, Murphy, O'Grady, John Horgan and

Brian Darrer were arrested and charged with conspiring to defraud bookmakers. Collins joined them. The case against O'Grady was subsequently dropped, but in February 1976, at Preston Crown Court, Murphy and Collins were both found guilty and fined £1,000 each. It was a cruel verdict, because the judge had summed up for an acquittal.

The Gay Future team got so much right, and a simple thing wrong. Collins should have loaded Opera Cloak and Ankerwyke into a horsebox, and arranged for it to break down; or, as he suggested to me later, put the horses somewhere safe and reported that they hadn't eaten up and couldn't race. Instead, the trainer left them grazing contentedly outside the window of his house in Troon. When someone phoned to ask where they were, Collins wasn't there to head off the danger, and the person who picked up the phone innocently told the caller that he could see the two horses from where he was standing. It was the prosecution's ability to convince the jury that Opera Cloak and Ankerwyke were never intended runners that spoiled the game.

The guilty verdict sealed the fate of all the betting slips with Gay Future's name written on them, and in 1977 the Jockey Club banned Collins and Murphy from British racecourses for ten years.

Within a month of his Cartmel victory, Gay Future was bought for a five-figure sum by – who else? – John Banks. It gave Banks yet more publicity, but Gay Future didn't win another race, and in January 1976 he belied his name by getting killed in a fall at Wetherby.

'Time heals,' Collins told me, 'but ten years is a long time. I didn't miss the training, but I missed going racing with friends. It was a savage sentence.'

When he finally returned to the racecourse, at his home course of Ayr, Collins' close friend Robert Sangster kept a long-standing promise to join him. Sangster did more. He named a racehorse after his friend and, when Colonel Collins

won a race at Newmarket in 1993, the man who trained Gay
Future was there to greet him.

The three years full-time research came to an end but my thesis
didn't. By autumn 1974 I had almost finished gathering information but I hadn't started writing it up, and writing it up was
a long and complex task.

Every year, two publications emerged from the Institute of
Historical Research: one was called *Theses in Progress*, and the
other, *Theses Completed*. The first was thick, and the second was
thin. I was not going to be one of the many who made up the
difference in thickness. I had no interest in taking up a career
or making money, but I was devoted to my research.

In October, I got a job in the Social Security offices in
Bradford. We were paid on Friday mornings, and so were the
unemployed. At lunchtime, we used to go and watch the strip-
per in a big pub on Manningham Lane. After she'd lost her
shirt, we went round the corner to Ladbrokes and lost ours. In
the evenings and at weekends I'd work on my thesis, but the
time was too fragmented, so I left Social Security and got a job
as a boardman with Ladbrokes. It paid £13 a week, and as
many marker pens as I could eat, and it left me the mornings
free to work on my thesis.

Occasionally I went back to Huntingdon, a trip too nostalgic
to be enjoyable, and I was there on 23 January 1975, when
Even Sail lined up for the start of the Wyton Handicap Chase.
There were just four runners for the three-mile event, and the
form book made Even Sail a hot favourite. Partnered by Tom
Jones's promising young son, Chris Thomson Jones, Even Sail
had won two of his last three races. Only Katie Gaze's useful
Even Dawn had got the better of him. That January day, many
racegoers went to Huntingdon with a vivid picture of Even Sail
in their minds. Just four weeks earlier, Even Sail had comfortably justified favouritism over the same course and distance.

Of his three opponents, Beau By could only have been in search of a safe journey and place money. It was the ten-year-old's third run of the season, and on both of his previous outings he had been pulled up. The season before, Peter Allingham's deteriorating chaser had run twice, and finished last twice. That left Josh Gifford's twelve-year-old, Avondhu, and Derek Ancil's six-year-old, Pava's Boy. Pava's Boy had bits of form to his name, but at Leicester in mid-December he had finished a long way behind Even Sail and a 9lb pull in the weights hardly seemed enough to bridge the gulf. Avondhu, a prolific winner over hurdles and fences in Ireland and England, had more to recommend him. The Wyton Handicap Chase represented a drop in class for him, but age was beginning to take its toll. Avondhu was losing his sparkle, while Even Sail was at the top of his form.

It was a most unusual race, for all the serious action took place before the runners had reached the first fence.

As the four horses walked around the paddock, managers at Hill's shops in York and Tadcaster reported big cash bets on Avondhu and Pava's Boy, in singles and reverse forecasts. On went the red lights. Hills contacted Ladbrokes, Corals and Mecca. Corals were already on their toes. 'There was too much interest in horses which seemed on the book unlikely to beat the favourite,' a spokesman said. 'We advised our betting shops and racecourse representatives to be extra cautious.' Ladbrokes got on the phone to 'blow' money back to the course for Avondhu and Pava's Boy. While Even Sail drifted from 7–4 on to 5–4 against, Avondhu and Pava's Boy moved in the opposite direction, from 5–2 to 11–8 and from 6–1 to 3–1. Beau By, at 33–1, was ignored.

To the right of the grandstand, at the three-mile start, the four runners lined up. As they galloped towards the first fence, Even Sail was pulled up. Avondhu strolled home a distance clear of Pava's Boy.

Chris Thomson Jones told the local stewards that, while adjusting his leathers at the start, he had inadvertently misplaced the holding pin. When Even Sail jumped off, the pin gave way. The stewards drew Thomson Jones's attention to his responsibility for seeing that the tack was in a fit condition for racing, and cautioned him.

That might have been the end of the matter, but there was the betting to explain. Those who banked on Even Sail's defeat won an estimated £7,000. That was a tidy sum in 1975, and the bookmakers reckoned that it would have been £50,000 if the alarm bells hadn't started ringing, and action been taken to shorten the starting prices.

By the time the police had been called in, Thomson Jones was in South Carolina, where he had taken a job as a work rider. 'We would very much like to see Mr Chris Thomson Jones,' said Detective Chief Inspector Strickland Carter, 'and I feel sure he is aware of this, but so far he has not contacted us.' In 1976, the Jockey Club invited Thomson Jones to appear at an inquiry into the Even Sail case; but when the enquiry opened on 8 September, Thomson Jones was not there to greet it. In his absence, the amateur rider was banned for seven years for deliberately preventing Even Sail from winning. Thomson Jones, it emerged, had made statements admitting the offence. Two years later, he returned to England, but was soon back in the United States. It was left to his brother, Tim, to win the amateur riders' championship.

The Ladbrokes shop I worked in was in Lidget Green, a ten-minute walk from Waverley Terrace. It was a small shop, and it has closed now. I used to stand on a narrow, raised platform behind the counter. Between races, I sat on a stool at one end of the platform. Under the stool was a bucket of bleached water, with my rags in it. I remember the smell of the bleach and the way it dried out your fingers. I remember the smoke, too. There was an extractor fan in the wall by the stool, but it didn't work. Every time the district manager paid a visit, I asked him if we could have it repaired. It never was. The district manager didn't want to talk about broken fans, or lunch arrangements, and Ladbrokes didn't want you to talk about them, either. Unions were anathema to them. What Ladbrokes wanted to talk about was turnover and multiple bets.

The manageress was a little Yorkshire terrier called Kath, who combined fierce loyalty to Ladbrokes with permanent despair at the unceasing demands they made on her. Someone smart and thrusting would call in to gear us up for the latest promotion, and when he had left Kath would sigh and say, 'Ooh, kid, bugger that for a game of soldiers.'

On Saturdays, I went in early because of the Hackney dogs, and Doris, the cashier, would go next door and fetch fish and chips. Once a week, Doris had a day off, and a relief cashier took her place. Sooner or later, she would disappear into the small washroom, and soon after that we would hear a steady humming noise. After a couple of weeks, I asked Kath what the noise was, and she told me. I couldn't help looking at the relief cashier afterwards, and wondering.

I enjoyed working as a boardman. You couldn't have a good betting shop without a good boardman. It was a source of pride to cope well with five race meetings, and to show you knew what the punters wanted. Good boardmen made sure they put up the going, and jockey changes, and overweights. I remember standing with the black and red and green marker pens in my hand. A lot of boardmen used to mark up the odds for the favourite in red, and the rest in black, but I didn't like that. To me, it seemed a touch insulting: 'There's the favourite, boys, off you go and do your money on it.' Speed and accuracy; in and out, back to the side, out of people's way. Take down the old marker sheet, stick two pieces of Sellotape to the bottom of the new one, to hold it flush against the white board; back on to the stool, drop the cloth into the bleached water, and listen to Kath telling one of the punters what was what. She was tough, Kath, and they loved her.

Any bet that took out more than £250 had to be reported. We didn't have any very big punters, just one man who'd have £40 win bets, always on a favourite. No bookmaker minds those. Keep them coming. If there was a bigger bet, Kath would stand the slip on the till in front of her, and keep picking it up and looking at it again, suspiciously. She didn't like her shop having to pay out. 'Ooh, kid.'

When I went home, my clothes stank of tobacco smoke, the punter's giveaway. If I die of lung cancer, that's what caused it.

While we were in Bradford, I started watching Doncaster Rovers again, although I was never a regular supporter. It was a good time to go, because by Rovers' standards, they had some great forwards. A pity about the backwards.

The Rovers were a fourth division side. They liked it there. Now and again, just to show willing, they got promoted, but it didn't suit them. As soon as they could, they slipped back down, and heaved a sigh of relief. Back with the clubs they loved; Stockport County, Crewe Alexandra, Hartlepool, Torquay United, Accrington Stanley and Gateshead, God rest their souls.

On the terraces, regulars talked about the season mirabilis, 1946/47, when the Rovers were League Division Three (North) champions. They won thirty-three of their forty-two games, lost just three, and scored 123 goals, with Clarrie Jordan netting forty-two of them. The year after, dizzied by Division Two, they won nine games, scored thirty-nine goals and went straight back down again.

When the terraces weren't reminiscing about 1947, they were remembering Alick Jeffrey, the best player Rovers never really had. Jeffrey made his debut as a fifteen-year-old in 1954, kicked off the 1956–7 season by scoring fifteen goals in thirteen games and then, still only seventeen, broke his leg badly when playing for the England Under-23 side against France. He would have been a great player, and Rovers' fans could never forget it. Told he would never play again, in 1963 Jeffrey made an emotional return to Belle Vue. It was my birthday, and much the biggest crowd of the season, over 11,000, turned out to see him. They wanted Alick Jeffrey to bring back a memory. I remember the cheers as he ran out, fatter than he should have been. Although Jeffrey wasn't the player he would have become, he still managed to score thirty-six goals the following season. Nowadays, he runs the Black Bull Hotel in the market place.

The Club didn't have tuppence to spend, but in the early 1970s the youth team came up with Mike Elwiss, later sold for a club record fee to Preston North End; Terry Curran, who disappeared to Nottingham Forest, thank God; Peter Kitchen, who ended up at Orient, and should have done better; and big Brendan O'Callaghan, who eventually lumbered down to Stoke City. In return for Curran, the Rovers got Ian Miller, who later helped Blackburn into the Premier Division. They could have had Tony Woodcock too, the future England international, but Rovers couldn't afford the £15,000 Nottingham Forest wanted, so they had him on loan instead.

These players weren't all in the Rovers' side at the same time, but for a while, the fans had the oh-so-rare joy of watching a second division forward line in a fourth division team, with Stan Anderson as one of the best managers Rovers ever had. A pity the Club wasn't as good as he was.

O'Callaghan was big and clumsy and, to start with, good with his head and clueless with his feet, but he slowly learnt how to lay the ball off, and the team played to his strengths. Kitchen linked up well with O'Callaghan, so that they were thought of as a double-act. He was nimble and had a couple of clever tricks on the ball which often got him past his man. Miller was one of the fastest wingers in the game, much better than Curran, who drove us mad by always taking on one too many defenders, never pausing to look up. Higher division clubs were supposed to have scouts. It took them a long time to spot what was happening at Doncaster, I expect they'd given up going there.

Rovers were an awful Cup team. They never did a thing. Not in the FA Cup, not in the League Cup; nothing, until 1975. That year, in the League Cup, they started by knocking out third division Grimsby, courtesy of a hat-trick from O'Callaghan. Then they knocked out unbeaten third division Crystal Palace, followed by fourth division Torquay. Over 20,000, including me, clogged up Belle Vue's black dust car park to see what they could do against second division Hull City. Kitchen scored after ten minutes, Hull equalised. O'Callaghan, of all people, crossed; Ray Ternent sent his head diving in to the ball. 2–1. Into the last eight; away to Tottenham Hotspur.

Arriving at White Hart Lane was a feeling you knew you'd only have once. Their fans were so dismissive, so arrogant. I was full of the secret knowledge that, fourth division or not, Kitchen, O'Callaghan and Miller would surprise them. God knows what they'd make of Doncaster's defence, if they could find it. Steve Reed, Stan Brookes; oh dear. How long would it take them to rumble us?

The quality of Rovers' attack knocked Spurs and their fans back a bit. Alan Murray put us ahead, but then Spurs scored twice to lead by a fragile 2–1 at half-time. After 52 minutes, Kitchen levelled. Then, disaster. Les Chappell made a dreadful backpass to Denis Peacock. Own goal. Chris Balderstone, who played football for Rovers and cricket for Leicestershire, immediately drove a tremendous shot at Spurs' goal, but Pat

Jennings pulled off a finger-tip save and, suddenly, everything was different.

It took Spurs a long time, but they finally realised just how exposed Rovers' flanks were. Ralph Coates and Jimmy Neighbour ran riot down the wings; Rovers' forwards were starved of possession. Thrashed 7–2, yet Doncaster's finest hour-and-a-half.

## Chapter Five

# The Best Racing in the World: Brighton

In 1976 I took a job as a Lecturer in Modern History at the Buckinghamshire College of Higher Education. The college was in a beautiful setting, at Newland Park, near the village of Chalfont St Giles. To start with I got digs in Chalfont St Peter, with Mrs Dobbs. Mrs Dobbs was old and frail and, like most people I met, thought I was a quiet, well-mannered, rather bookish young man.

There was a small dive of a betting shop in Chalfont St Peter and, on 6 May 1976, I was banned from it. It was one of my proudest moments. I had won about £80; a lot more than it sounds today, but not a fortune. What really riled the bookmaker was that I had won it from an each-way bet on an 11–1 shot, Marie Louise, in a maiden race where they were betting evens the favourite, 8–1 bar. Bookmakers hate taking each-way bets in races where there is a short-priced favourite and all bar one or two are showing at long odds. This was the second time I had done it, and won, in the space of a few days.

When I walked up to the counter, a podgy, grumpy-faced

man gave me an unfriendly stare and said, 'I don't want any more of your bets.'

'Why not?'

'You know why.'

'No, I don't.' Although, of course, I did.

He tapped the slip with a stubby finger. 'Each-way bets when the favourite's odds-on, you know.' He made it sound immoral, criminal, a low trick.

'But if you let me carry on betting here, you're bound to get it all back.'

'No. That's it. I don't want your business.'

Which was a nuisance, because the next betting shop was in Gerrards Cross. So I went to Gerrards Cross a few times, had a little winning streak, nothing much, and they banned me from there, too.

If I was so bloody good, why was I always skint?

At least, as Rex Harrison said in *Dr Doolittle*, and he never said a truer word even if someone had written it for him, I had my health. If you ain't got that, you ain't got nothin'.

The Duke had his health, but insisted on doing what he could to ruin it. That April, Liverpool's Walton Hospital issued a bulletin. It read: 'The Duke's fracture of the right thigh bone and concussion have been dealt with and he is conscious and comfortable. It is hoped he will be fit to travel within a few days.' The Duke was the Duke of Alburquerque and the right thigh bone was the one he had broken when Nereo fell at the thirteenth fence in the Grand National. The Duke was fifty-seven at the time, and already had one metal plate in his leg, secured with seven screws. Together, Nereo and the Spanish Duke created a unique niche in the history of the National, and after I joined the *Sporting Life* I asked John Clark, who spoke Spanish, to phone the Duke and ask him about his National experiences.

'When I was eight,' the Duke told John, 'I went to the cinema in Madrid and watched a newsreel. It was about the Grand National, and it was the most exciting thing I had ever seen. From that moment on I was determined to ride in the race; it was my obsession.

'My family had horses and I went to France, to Pau and Paris, to ride in steeplechases, but always I was building up to the National.'

In the late 1940s the Duke of Alburquerque finally came to England and put horses in training, first with John Goldsmith and then with Peter Cazalet. It was Cazalet who trained the Duke's first Grand National runner, Brown Jack III. It was 1952 and the Duke was a mere thirty-three; when Brown Jack III fell at the fourth fence his rider broke two vertebrae and put in his first appearance at Liverpool's Walton Hospital. Before long, this unnaturally brave nobleman would know the casualty ward so well that he could have found his way there unaided, if it hadn't been for the fractures.

The vertebrae healed but it was 1963 before the Duke found another unsuitable mount. Jonjo fell at the twenty-first; the Duke of Alburquerque fell with him. Two years later Groomsman took a heavy fall at Valentine's Brook. The Duke broke a leg, bringing his career tally of fractures to twenty-two. The year after, 1966, it was Toby Balding's turn to give the intrepid Duke his instructions on L'Empereur. This wasn't easy. 'If he didn't want to listen to you,' Balding remembered, 'he suddenly wouldn't understand any English.'

Tall as a telegraph pole, the Duke was called on to ride at 10st 2lb, and answered the call. 'He rode with a pair of irons attached to the tree of a fibreglass saddle,' said Balding, incredulously. 'For him, it was a tremendous challenge. He was a total kamikaze pilot and brave as a lion.' A worrying combination.

L'Empereur pulled up four fences from home. Getting closer. And getting older. 'I didn't have the horses for the race,' said the Duke, ruefully. 'And then I bred Nereo.'

He sent Nereo to Fred Winter, a man who became his hero. 'Fred is a very, very great friend of mine. A great person; a giant among jockeys and among English sporting men.'

In 1970, Nereo made his debut in an amateur riders' hurdle race at Hereford. The long-faced Spaniard was on board and Nereo romped home. This was the horse to fulfil his dream. Two years later the Duke won his first chase on Nereo, at Sandown, and in 1973 he lined up for his fifth attempt at the National: a fifty-four-year-old jockey on a seven-year-old horse.

Winter had another horse in the race, called Crisp. While Crisp was taking our breath away, the Duke of Alburquerque was fighting his own battle, with a broken stirrup leather. He fought until the Canal Turn, and then surrendered. For once, the Duke emerged unscathed, and he drove back to Lambourn with Fred Winter. 'Fred never said a word, all the way back from Liverpool,' the Duke told John Clark, 'but when we arrived at Lambourn we had the most wonderful meal I have ever had in my life. There was champagne and caviar; it was party time. And that is what made Fred so great; he was such a brilliant loser.'

On to 1974: annus mirabilis. Forget about Red Rum, shout, shout for Nereo.

The Duke walked with Fred Winter into the paddock. 'Fred was always livid with me,' he remembered. 'He was furious that I was riding in the race and his instructions were monosyllabic.' Fred's temper wasn't helped by the fact that, a week before, the Duke had broken his collarbone at Newbury. He had also just had sixteen screws taken out of an injured leg. When the Duke fell, he tended to break something, because he was the wrong shape to emerge intact. 'His height was against him,' said Diana Winter. 'People that tall don't fall very well, they tend to splatter. He was a terribly brave man, such a great trier.'

'Ironically,' said the Duke, 'my best performance in the National was when I was in the worst condition. The poor animal had to do everything on his own. He didn't have a jockey on board but a sack of potatoes.'

The fifty-five-year-old potatoes rode extraordinarily well and Nereo came back a splendid eighth of the seventeen finishers. 'It gave me enormous satisfaction,' the Duke recalled, 'and if I had been in decent shape we wouldn't have been far away.' The British racegoers loved him.

Back in Seville, our hero suffered multiple compound fractures of his right leg. Even the Duke of Alburquerque could not ignore that, and he had to miss the 1975 version of the National. The following year, Nereo and the Duke were back again, fresh from victory at Sandown and on their way to Walton Hospital. 'Falling is purely a question of bad luck,' he told John, unconvincingly. 'The thing about bad luck is that it happens once and you don't expect it to happen again. The trouble is that I was always far too excited.'

The next year produced a different kind of excitement. Early in 1977 the Duke travelled to London to hear the Stewards of the Jockey Club announce that they were not prepared to renew the fifty-eight-year-old's riding permit. He was outraged. 'I was absolutely furious,' he said, fifteen years later, as if still trying to contain his anger. 'I was in brilliant physical condition. I had trained hard and I was ready to ride. I couldn't understand the doctor's decision. It was my body, my horse and my responsibility.'

Fred Winter was not outraged. He said at the time, 'I am both very sad and very relieved.'

Reluctantly, the Duke of Alburquerque was forced to be intrepid elsewhere. In 1991, at the age of seventy-two, this remarkable man completed the 721 kilometre pilgrimage to Santiago da Compostela, on foot. But his thoughts were elsewhere, at Aintree, and the Walton Hospital. 'I spent most of my time unconscious, but when I did wake up, the staff were always charming.'

They loved him, too. 'Every year,' recalled John Thomson, the medical director, 'the staff would say, "Oh, I wonder if we'll be seeing the Duke this year?" ' He rarely disappointed them.

The Duke of Alburquerque, the one and only, died in 1994, aged seventy-five.

While other people talked about Royal Ascot and Glorious Goodwood, Ian Carnaby and I wallowed in the delights of Royal Windsor and Glorious Brighton. Windsor always held an evening meeting on the Monday before Royal Ascot; I went for the first time in 1976, and I still love those Monday evening meetings.

On your way in, as you turn right at the mini-roundabout into Mill Lane, the Swan pub is on your left. At least, it used to be a pub, until they improved it. Somewhere in the improving the barman got lost, which was a shame, because I liked being served by him. I think he was only blind in one eye. Anyway, he knew when you were there and had a pretty good idea where the glasses were. After that, everything became a bit uncertain. You just had to hope for a pint of the best. He used to hold his head at an angle, like Henry Cecil, and squint at the glass with his half-good eye, as if he didn't believe the evidence of his own hand. Then he'd start pulling. When he thought the glass was full, he'd put it on the counter, feel for the rim and dip a finger in, just to make sure.

After pausing here, Ian and I used to walk down the road to the racecourse. If it was the second Monday in July, we'd spend our time thinking hard about the six-furlong apprentice selling handicap. On the face of it, this was a pretty silly thing to do. There were always at least eighteen runners, one of the two I fancied was always badly drawn and the other one was ridden by an apprentice I'd never heard of. No one had heard of him.

He wasn't sure who he was himself. I went to that meeting for almost twenty years, and never once backed the winner of the apprentice race. One year, I bumped into the winning rider.

'Well done,' I said.

'Thank you,' he replied, with a broad grin. 'We were a bit naughty with it last time.'

That sort of thing is all very well, as long as someone tells me about it. Which reminds me of a race at Windsor in 1985, when Philip Waldron gave Tracing a most interesting ride. Two weeks later, they were both back. Times were hard, rock hard. I managed to get in but there was nothing left to buy a betting slip with. Tracing opened at 33–1, closed at 10–1 and strolled in by eight lengths. Geoff Lewis, the trainer, told the stewards that he had been reluctant to be hard on the three-year-old in his previous races because of the colt's wind problems. 'I think he'll go on from here,' said Geoff. He did.

I'm not complaining. You can't if you were there that day in 1976 when Wenallt Red Knight carried Des Cullen through the running rail and on into the River Thames. The water was only 3ft 6in deep, which would have been fine except that Cullen measured 3ft 3in and couldn't swim. His feet touched the bottom, but unfortunately his head didn't touch the top. Luckily, someone got him out. I wish they'd done the same for me.

For years, they've had a racecard competition at Windsor, sponsored by Lanson Champagne. You have to name the first three home in the third race, and the prize is twelve bottles of bubbly. I managed to win the competition three times, which should bring hope to everyone. The last time, they were going to take my photograph for a brochure, but I think they were put off by the holes in my jeans.

There used to be a good system at Windsor; Ian swore by it. Back the favourite in the last. Then stroll down to the Swan. I wish that barman was still there.

I wish Robert Morley was still there, too. Morley's unmistakable profile was often on display at Windsor. He used to potter along to the evening meetings from his home at Crazies Hill, near Henley. I visited him there once – a lovely, unserious, mild, witty, whimsical man; one of those rare people who, within a minute, you like enormously. I can picture Morley now, sitting in a deckchair at the bottom of his long garden, a scrapbook on his lap and a cigar in his mouth, talking about the theatre, and racing, and his time as a racehorse owner with his great friend and fellow actor, Wilfrid Hyde-White. Morley was eighty-three when I met him. 'No, I don't go to the theatre any more,' he told me, 'but I go to the occasional memorial service.'

He was about to go to one in memory of Hyde-White, one of the Turf's most enthusiastic and endearing supporters. During the 1960s and early 1970s, Morley and Hyde-White had horses in training with Ian Walker. Some of them, like Soft Collar, Lend An Ear and Three Sevens, were quite successful.

'Nearly all our horses won – once,' Morley remarked, in his wonderfully wry way. 'They weren't monotonous winners. Wilfrid used to put £1,000 on every time one of our horses ran, but it became difficult for the bookmakers to compete with the Inland Revenue.'

Hyde-White, the quintessential English gentleman who had appeared in classic films such as *The Third Man* and *My Fair Lady*, was far more interested in racing than in the cinema. When a visitor asked him whether he ever watched his old movies, Hyde-White looked appalled. 'Good God, no. I'm not as ill as that.'

Putting £1,000 on every time one of his horses ran didn't do much for Hyde-White's solvency, but led to some famous appearances in the London Bankruptcy Court. The official receiver once asked this lovable character, 'Why are you staying at the Savoy Hotel?'

Hyde-White replied, 'Two reasons, dear chap. One, it is the finest hotel in London and, two, it is the nearest to Carey Street.'

'But how are you going to pay for it?'

'Well, you're the financial expert, you tell me.'

During another bankruptcy hearing, the receiver said to Hyde-White, 'If you cannot tell us how you spent such a large sum in so short a time, perhaps you could tell us what will win the Gold Cup at Ascot this afternoon?' Hyde-White found that question much easier to answer than the previous ones.

'Only have a small bet, though,' he advised the receiver. 'We don't want to have to change places, do we?'

Tax problems encouraged Hyde-White to move to California, but when Royal Ascot came round, he used to be there in spirit, dressing up in top hat and tails, complete with carnation. Even when life seemed to have little to offer, Wilfrid faced it with wit. 'The only companion I have now,' he remarked in old age, 'is a Yugoslavian cook, and she is trying to poison me.'

Morley and Hyde-White had a lot in common, and when Hyde-White disappeared to America, Morley briefly followed him. His English gentleman's voice was in great demand. 'I had my own programme there called *Celebrity Chefs*,' Morley told me. 'The celebrities cooked something and I added the salt.' Back in Britain, Morley discovered the joys of television commercials. 'It was better than the cinema; you didn't have to get up so early. British Airways was the best. They used to say, "I'm sorry, Mr Morley, but we can't get into the Ritz for lunch today. Will the Dorchester be all right?" '

Morley bought his first racehorse in the flush of funds from his first play, *Edward, My Son*. He called the horse The Gloomy Sentry, after a line in the play, and sent it to be trained by Evan Williams, at Kingsclere in Berkshire. 'Williams was a bit classy for me. He eventually gave up training because his wife couldn't bear to meet the owners.' One day in 1951, Morley went to Worcester with Williams and heard him utter the unforgettable words, 'We're going in.' 'It was wonderful to stand in the winner's enclosure after having done absolutely nothing.'

When Hyde-White was no longer in a fit financial condition to own racehorses, Morley became a sole owner, with Freddie Maxwell and Ray Laing being awarded the pleasure of training them. Morley's best day as an owner was at Epsom in 1984, when Bobby Dazzler won. 'Ray Laing didn't think he had any chance, so I backed him at 12–1.'

Appropriately, it was a selling race at Windsor in 1988 which provided Morley with his final success, when Class Struggle paid for the caviar and cigars at 14–1. On its previous outing, Class Struggle had finished almost last. 'No one asked for an explanation,' Morley recalled, 'which was just as well, because I certainly couldn't have given one.

'I have always liked it at Windsor. It's so dilapidated. They announce tremendous plans and then plant another patch of grass in the car park. And I like the selling races there. I once tried to get John Huston to buy a horse out of a seller. I said, "Bid for it, John," and the horse fell down dead.'

I don't know if Robert Morley ever visited Brighton, but he would have liked it. To get the best out of a day at Brighton races, you have to arrive early. Drive straight down to the sea, stop before you get there, and turn left. Half a mile along the seafront there is a lovely pitch-and-putt golf course with a café where they do a nice line in breakfasts and pretty waitresses. I've always been very successful with the breakfasts.

If you are too late for golf, at least make sure you have time to stop off at a little country pub on the Sussex Downs. Order a pint of dry cider and a ploughman's lunch, and sit down to work out what is going to win the selling race. The first time you work your way through the form, you'll be convinced that none of them can win it. They're not good enough. Have another look. One of them's got to win. It won't be the one you choose, but that isn't the point. It is better to have bet and lost than never to have bet at all.

When you've found the sea, turn round and head straight up

the steep hill. Near the top is a Ladbrokes shop for punters who have spent so long in betting shops that they think that's where racing happens. Besides, by saving the price of admission, they can have another losing treble. When you can't climb any higher, you have reached Brighton racecourse. This is the place that Graham Greene wrote about in *Brighton Rock*, with its race-gangs and small-time crooks. The gangs have long gone, and so has one of the grandstands. Luckily, there is a spare one and, when you climb up it, the view is wonderful – unless there happens to be a sea fret, in which case there is a wonderful view of the fret.

Fret permitting, across to the right you can see the sea and across to the left a racetrack like no other. The one-and-a-half-mile start lies way up high on the edge of the Downs, and half a mile out the runners turn sharp left and pour helter-skelter downhill into a deep hollow before scooting uphill to the finish. The steep hill was introduced in order to give the slower horses a chance to build up a bit of speed, because the standard of racing here is what is politely called 'moderate'. It doesn't matter. If you took the runners from a Brighton seller, changed their names, switched the race to Epsom and called it the Derby, most people wouldn't notice the difference.

When the runners eventually pass the post you will want to know what to do while other people are collecting their winnings. If you like a challenge, you could try to get a drink. In Tattersalls, one of the bars has all the pipes and pumps stuck up on the wall, like intestines worn on the outside. Downstairs, opposite the racecourse betting shop, you can get jellied eels.

A man in a wheelchair used to spend the whole afternoon wheeling himself backwards and forwards in front of the betting shop screens, crushing people's toes. Personally, I prefer to stay in the stand and watch other people. If you like men with huge beer bellies, this is the racecourse for you. We have competitions to see who can spot the biggest belly on parade.

Believe me, madam, you wouldn't want to be lying under the winner. Brighton bellies. Big ones, huge ones, ones hanging over waistbands in the afternoon sun. Bellies carried in front of their backward-leaning owners.

A bottle of champagne on one of the white tables out in the sun between the parade ring and the course, just mulling things over, chatting idly. It's bliss.

Don't forget to keep a record of your losers. When you have had six, the racing is over. Don't go home, though. Go into Brighton, instead. Easy-going Brighton. There are some great pubs and restaurants, but you have to be a bit careful. I once strolled into a pub and ordered two beers. The looks seemed a bit out of the ordinary, and then I glanced up at the walls. They were covered with pictures of men's bottoms. I didn't want mine on the wall, so we moved on to the Chequers, an old haunt near Regency Square. They have a sign there that reads, 'No Shirt. No Shoes. No Serve.' Two women were kissing at the bar. A man was dancing to a Billy Fury record. Brighton's like that. No one cares.

# Chapter Six

# Gladioli and Lobsters

One day, instead of turning left at the end of the lane from the college, towards the village of Chalfont St Giles, I turned right, down Nightingales Lane, towards Little Chalfont. On either side of the road was woodland, with large, settled houses glimpsed between hedges and sycamores. I turned into one of the drives, and tried to imagine what Hermit's Wood had been like in the 1940s and 1950s, when Dorothy Wyndham Paget lived there.

Miss Paget was the owner of Golden Miller, the only serious rival to Arkle for the title of best steeplechaser ever. Golden Miller won five successive Cheltenham Gold Cups during the 1930s, and remains the only horse to have won the Gold Cup and Grand National in the same year, 1934.

The house hadn't changed much since 1960, when Dorothy Paget died. There was a lodge at the entrance, painted white, where Mr Hall, the gardener and odd-job man, used to live. At the side was a shed with a heated floor, installed for the comfort of Miss Paget's Great Danes. At the back of the house was a balcony leading to the room where Dorothy lived, ate and telephoned, and from which her instructions were issued. When the present occupant, Tina Watson, arrived the lawn was in a dreadful state, because Hall was rarely allowed to cut the grass during the day, when Miss Paget was asleep, and it was difficult to cut it at night, when she was awake. 'Tell Hall to grow gladioli,' Paget would say, and the message would reach him through a network of duplicated notes and secretaries. Each secretary was allotted a colour – blue, yellow or pink – to identify both the secretary and her notes.

In the village, Hall was known as 'the eunuch', because the villagers couldn't believe that Miss P would allow an 'entire' on the premises. All her other staff, including drivers and mechanics, were women. Dorothy didn't like men. She told her cousin that the worst experience of her life was being kissed by a drunken Frenchman, and she didn't rate sober Englishmen much more highly. When wartime regulations prevented her from reserving a whole railway carriage for herself, she appealed to the Minister of Transport to exempt her from the restriction, on the ground that sitting next to strange men made her vomit. She did what she could to put them off, with great success. Burdened with a large, round, flat-fronted face, Miss P never wore make-up and her favoured costume was a Girl-Guide-like beret and long, shapeless, tweed coat. When she greeted Golden Miller in the winner's enclosure with a kiss, one wag remarked that it was the first time she had ever kissed a member of the opposite sex. To be fair to her, not many of her suitors had won a Gold Cup.

Dorothy Paget and Golden Miller had little in common, although Golden Miller also ate like a horse. In her younger days, Dorothy had been an accomplished horsewoman, riding side-saddle in point-to-points. Later, though, she discovered food and ate it on a scale which few others have been able to emulate until it was impossible to imagine her – more than twenty stones of her – on horseback. (The RSPCA was founded in 1824.) Few people visited Hermit's Wood, but the house still boasted a day cook, a night cook, and a lot of larders.

When Dorothy ventured out, she took precautions to avoid too much unwelcome human contact. If she wanted to see a film, she booked the whole of Amersham cinema. If she went out to dinner, she was likely to arrive with a thermos flask and a pack of sandwiches. At Wimbledon she booked two seats, one for herself and the other for her handbag. When she went to vote, Miss P took her own pencil. 'In case the horrible socialists should have stolen the public pencils.'

By chance, I met Alice Wilson, who ran a taxi service in Little Chalfont during the war. Alice used to pick Mr Hall up from Hermit's Wood every day and take him to collect 'The Pink 'Un.' The job came to an abrupt end when Mrs Wilson's dog sank its canines into one of the secretary's legs. The crime was not to have bitten her leg but to have bitten the stocking that surrounded it. 'It was the only house in Chalfont with stockings,' Alice explained. 'Dorothy Paget had hers specially made. She had the most enormous legs. No ordinary stockings would fit her.'

Strangers were strongly discouraged from visiting Hermit's Wood, and even members of her family were not encouraged. Dorothy fell out with her father and sister, who lived in Leeds Castle in Kent with a son glorying in the name of Sir Gawaine George Hope Baillie. When I phoned Sir Gawaine, Dorothy's nephew, he told me that he had only met her twice. 'My mother and her sister didn't get on.'

Nor did most people, which seemed to suit the eccentric, frequently unpleasant, but enormously rich Miss Paget. When you know that you are going to be given over £1 million, on the sole condition that you keep breathing until 1926 arrives, along with your twenty-first birthday, pleasing other people becomes an optional extra. Miss P gave it a very low priority. A higher priority, once her inheritance was safely in her hand-bag, was to set about spending it. Dorothy flirted briefly with motor racing (exciting but no betting), before alighting on horseracing (exciting and with betting). Miss P embraced the blank-cheque approach to bloodstock investment, and chalked up some spectacularly bad buys before spending £12,000 on Insurance, who went on to win the Champion Hurdle in 1932 and 1933, and Golden Miller.

Dorothy declared herself 'terribly pleased' with Golden Miller's Gold Cup–Grand National double, and awarded large chocolate effigies of her champion to the trainer, Basil Briscoe, jockey, Gerry Wilson, and head lad. They deserved their reward, for Miss Paget's daily routine started with dinner at 7.00 a.m., followed by bedtime, followed by breakfast at 8.30 p.m., when her day began. She had an insatiable appetite for discussing her horses with her trainers, and liked to open the debate at about 10.30 p.m. On one occasion she despatched a messenger to Briscoe at 2.30 in the morning, to instruct him to replace the telephone receiver which he had taken off the hook in a vain attempt to claim some sleep.

Briscoe was not temperamentally equipped to deal with Paget's eccentric and despotic ways, and nor were many of the other sixteen English trainers selected for the mixed blessing of her patronage. Fulke Walwyn, who trained more winners for Miss P than anyone else, among them Mont Tremblant, the winner of the 1952 Gold Cup, eventually lost patience and diplomatically suggested a change of trainer.

'She kept such funny hours,' Walwyn told me, 'and was always ringing up. She was a difficult person, so trying, and eventually I got fed up with her constant phone calls and resigned.'

Paget rarely visited her trainers; during the five years Gordon Richards trained for her, she failed to put in a single appearance. This was just as well, because she was habitually unpunctual. An outing to the races was preceded by a frenzy of notes and instructions. Watches were tuned in to Greenwich Mean Time, a precaution which failed to get Dorothy to the racecourse on time, and Hall was told to stand in the middle of Nightingales Lane to keep oncoming traffic at bay, so that Miss P could accelerate uninterrupted out of the drive. On one occasion, her car broke down, forcing Miss P to proceed to the racecourse in a butcher's delivery van, which she had purchased on the spot. After that, a second car always followed her, as a reserve, with a third car joining the convoy on long journeys. She rarely arrived in time to savour the paddock preliminaries, but this didn't trouble her; she was much more interested in the look of the betting market.

Dorothy was a disciplined gambler, betting only from Monday to Saturday. Most of her bets ranged from the equivalent of a modest semi to that of a substantial estate. She would start at £1,000 and work her way steadily up to a reputed lifetime best of £160,000. (On an 8–1 on shot. It won.) One of her biggest bets was on Colonel Payne in the 1939 Cork and Orrery Stakes at Royal Ascot. Fred Darling, the horse's trainer, had made encouraging noises about Colonel Payne's chance, and Dorothy had acted on them, to excess. When Gordon Richards and Colonel Payne returned to the unsaddling enclosure, soundly beaten, Miss P was there to greet them. 'Where's Mr Darling?' she demanded. 'I wouldn't be quite sure, Miss Paget,' Richards replied, 'but I've a shrewd idea he's on the top of the stand, cutting his throat.'

As time went by, the expanding Miss Paget went racing less, but bet more. Since she tended to be in bed, asleep, during racing hours, she had a unique arrangement with her bookmaker, who allowed her to bet after the racing was over.

'I'll have £400 on the favourite in the first.'

'Very good, Miss Paget. I'm afraid that one let you down.'

For most of us, it is the only system that would offer a

fighting chance of making racing pay, but Miss P still managed to lose houses on a regular basis.

In 1939 Golden Miller joined Insurance in retirement at Paget's Elsenham Stud Farm in Essex. Unlike their owner, they both lived to a ripe old age, dying within three months of each other, both aged thirty, in 1957. Dorothy Paget did not long outlive the horse who made her famous. At her death, aged fifty-four, she left no last will and testament, just 'The Heaps': piles of notes and fading copies of the *Sporting Life*.

There were a lot of second-hand furniture shops in Bradford. One day, I bought a plain, solid, rectangular table for £4. We put it in the converted loft, by the window overlooking the disused railway line. After we'd moved to Buckinghamshire, it sat in my room upstairs in the house at Wooburn Green – and I sat with it, sharpening a particular make of HB pencil with a particular metal pencil sharpener, writing on W. H. Smith's narrow-lined, A4 paper; crossing it out, and writing it again.

I took time out to write a piece on 'The Urban Poor Law', but that made me even more anxious to finish the thesis. Finishing wasn't enough; it had to be finished to my satisfaction, and that was a painstaking, time-consuming job. It was taking too long so, in 1978, I decided to go on the dole for six months and finish it. Everybody, sensibly, advised me against this. Even Dr Fraser wrote, urging the importance of 'being in work', but finishing the thesis meant a lot to me, having a job and earning money didn't.

During the summer, I hired a van and drove over to Reading with a friend. We knocked on front doors, or back doors, asking people if they had any bicycles they wanted to sell. It's a depressing experience, knocking on doors in the evening, because what you see is isolated groups of people sitting watching television. There's something surreal and sad about it. But filling the van with bicycles was easy. Then we drove back to Wooburn Green and put the bikes in the garage. That summer, I tinkered with them in the sunshine by the back door, with Oliver and Richard.

My wife had discovered a scheme which allowed white, middle-class liberals, like us, to have a teenager from a deprived, inner-city home for a holiday. The beauty of it was that you only had to have your visitor for a couple of weeks, but you could tell everyone you'd done it for years afterwards.

We had Richard, from somewhere unpleasant in London. As soon as he arrived in the bedroom, Richard picked up a guitar, swung it around his head a few times, and then started to bang it against the wall. We spent a lot of time trying to stop Richard killing either children or bicycles. I didn't mind the children; it was the bicycles that worried me. After carefully examining my principles, I used to chase him down the road, shouting, 'Come here, you little bugger.'

I was doing quite well with the bikes. Then, one day, a few minutes after I'd sold one, there was a knock at the door. It was the man who'd just bought the bike. One of the pedals had fallen off, and so had he. 'I could have been killed,' he said. I realised he was right, and that my future didn't lie in bicycles.

Even with them, there was more time to devote to my thesis, and more time to devote to the form. Life revolved around the piles of notes on the table in my study and the pages of the *Sporting Life*. The *Sporting Life* revealed that on 17 August 1978 Lorna Vincent scrambled home on Pretty Cute at Devon and Exeter, at 25–1. It was the nineteen-year-old's first ride over jumps. I noticed it then, and remember it now, because Lorna Vincent was one of the first women professional jump jockeys, the best, and the most enduring. People forget how good she was. Lorna finished that season with an impressive tally of fifteen wins from seventy-four mounts, and the following year bettered it with twenty-two wins from just 109 rides. That is still a record for the number of winners over jumps by a woman rider, and it was gained at a time when there was widespread prejudice against women jockeys. None of the five riders above her in the junior riders' table that season was able to match Lorna's 20 per cent strike rate; the five were Richard Rowe, Chris Grant, Hywel Davies, Peter Scudamore and Phil Tuck.

What made Lorna's success even more remarkable was that it was achieved without the support of a racing family. As a schoolgirl, Lorna shared the popular dream of becoming a top-class show-jumper. The dream faded into fantasy when her parents split up, her pony died, and her mother told her it was time to become a secretary and earn some dinner money. Instead, Lorna resolved to find work in a yard, any yard, and save up to buy her own horse. She pulled out the Yellow Pages and came across an entry that read 'L. Kennard. Racehorse trainer.' A week later, she was working for him.

Still there was no thought of becoming a jockey. 'I was happy looking after the horses,' Lorna told me, years later. 'I loved riding out and schooling but race-riding didn't appeal to me.'

In 1977, Les Kennard persuaded Lorna to make her race-course debut, in a Flat race at Bath. Officially, Fast Flo slipped up after two furlongs; unofficially, says Vincent, 'The boys were out to get me and they turned me upside down. As far as they were concerned, it wasn't a girl's game, you were taking their rides, and that was that.' When she met Kennard on the miserable walk back and told him what had happened, he advised her to keep quiet, or she'd have trouble for ever after.

Kennard was often criticised for his treatment of jockeys – the *Sporting Life*'s Geoff Lester once wrote, 'Kennard goes through jockeys faster than Britt Ekland does boyfriends' – but he was a rare judge of riding ability, and very few trainers would have given Vincent the opportunities Kennard gave her. Lorna seized her chances on decent horses like Gently Does It and Walnut Wonder, but the partnership came to a very public end in 1981. Walnut Wonder had been laid out for a gamble in the Lanzarote Handicap Hurdle at Kempton. Lorna had ridden the six-year-old in his four build-up runs; she knew the plan, and she went to Kempton expecting to execute it. But when she got there, Kennard told her that he was putting Anthony Webber on board. Backed from 14–1 to 7–1, Walnut Wonder duly hacked up. For Lorna, instead of celebrations, there were tears and recriminations.

After the split, Vincent got work riding out for small West Country trainers like Billy Williams and Arthur Barrow, but there were few rides and fewer winners. For several seasons, Lorna hovered just above rock bottom, until 1985–6, when she hit it. Her score sheet read 'zero'. Instead of quietly fading away, Lorna battled on, working hard to get more rides. 'I rode work all over the place, for tiny little trainers no one had ever heard of, living in the hope that, one day, out of one of those small yards, a nice horse would come along.' The talent didn't go away, nor the determination. Two broken legs and a broken nose couldn't dampen Vincent's enthusiasm, and in the end it was rewarded.

When Mick Channon took his own battered legs off the football pitch and turned himself into a successful trainer, Lorna Vincent became his assistant. In the 1990–1 jumps season, she finally got back into double figures. She did it again the following year and even rode a couple of winners on the Flat. By 1994 the other young riders she once matched, Richard Rowe and Peter Scudamore, Hywel Davies, Chris Grant and Phil Tuck, had all cleaned their racing boots for the last time. Lorna Vincent kept going, and is still going, in the United States.

Eleven days after Lorna made headlines on Pretty Cute, In The Money set off to make his own fame. Ridden by John Williams, In The Money won the Hatherleigh Selling Handicap Hurdle at Newton Abbot by twenty lengths, having been backed from 20–1 to 8–1. Trained by John Bowles at

Crickhowell in Powys, the nine-year-old had last run in November 1975, when he was pulled up. He had never completed the course over jumps and had one undistinguished performance on the Flat to his name. Bowles told the curious stewards that In The Money had a history of breaking blood vessels and had broken down when raced in 1975. The stewards 'recorded' his explanation, a sign that they weren't convinced.

The following day, In The Money was put down. Williams testified that he had felt In The Money's leg go at the second last hurdle, although the horse looked sound at the post-race auction, when Bowles bought him back for 1,100 guineas. Yet according to Bowles, when In The Money got home, he 'could hardly hobble'. He took him to Lawrence Potter's Bristol slaughterhouse, where one of Potter's employees, Simon Chidzey, shot him.

While Bowles pleaded his innocence, Racecourse Security Services were busy examining photographs and taking evidence. Jeffrey Kear, one of Salaman's lads who knew In The Money, and knew that both the horse's front legs had been acid-fired, was at Newton Abbot and did not believe that the horse who won the race was In The Money. The racecourse vet, who examined the winner, saw no evidence of firing, but noticed a thickening of the tendon on the left foreleg. Colin Wallace, a racecourse photographer, had taken a number of pictures of the winner, who reminded him strongly of a horse he had once owned, Cobbler's March. He had photographs of that horse, too. Cobbler's March had been operated on for a tendon injury to his left fore, leaving the tendon thickened. There were other identifying marks which led the RSS and police to conclude that the horse who won at Newton Abbot was not In The Money but Cobbler's March.

Cobbler's March was an eleven-year-old who had not run since December 1976. Latterly, he had been lightly raced and his form was poor, but he was a better horse than In The Money and had won several small hurdle races for Earl Jones, Tommy Craig and Walter Charles. In September 1977 Bowles had bought him at the Ascot Sales for 620 guineas. Cobbler's March was never found. Bowles said that he had died of a twisted gut and been chopped up and fed to pigs and dogs.

In 1980 Bowles and Williams appeared at Exeter Crown Court, charged with conspiracy to defraud and deception. Williams was acquitted on all charges; Bowles was found guilty of dishonestly obtaining prize money from Weatherbys and the proceeds of a bet with the Tote by falsely claiming that the horse was In The Money. He was sentenced to nine months' imprisonment, suspended for two years, fined £750 on each charge and ordered to pay £1,500 costs. Later that year, the Jockey Club declared Bowles a disqualified person for twenty years.

Early in September 1978, I walked over to the betting shop on Wooburn Green, and had £20 each way on Julio Mariner at 66–1 for the St Leger.

Mainly, it was the breeding. I refused to believe that a horse by Blakeney out of Set Free, a brother to the Oaks and Irish Oaks winner Juliette Marny, wouldn't appreciate the Leger trip. If he did, and had one of his on days instead of his off ones, 66–1 was a silly price.

Julio Mariner had some good form to his name, and some bad form. On his seasonal debut, he had finished second to Shirley Heights in the Mecca-Dante Stakes at York and was then beaten eight lengths into sixth place in the Derby. After running rank badly in the King Edward VII Stakes at Royal Ascot, Julio Mariner was switched back to a mile to win a conditions race at York where the conditions were in his favour. A mile, for heaven's sake. Ridden up with the pace again in the Benson & Hedges Gold Cup at York over one and a quarter miles, the blinkered Julio Mariner faded badly behind

Hawaiian Sound. He went into the St Leger disappointing, inconsistent, bred to stay but yet to show that he did.

But I wasn't the only one who thought he might be the fly in the cold cream. On the day of the race, Clive Brittain's colt was backed from 40–1 to 28–1. I watched it at home on television. Held up, Julio Mariner was always going well for Eddie Hide behind a strong pace. He made up ground without faltering, and went into the lead a furlong out. Le Moss stayed on behind him, but was never going to get there.

In the evening, I started to think of lobster. I'd never eaten lobster in my life but decided I was going to eat lobster that night. I rang up some friends and then rang up a posh restaurant in a place called Fingest. Yes, sir, fresh lobster was on the menu. And so was lobster bisque. It was one of the starters. Might as well go the whole lobster and have that as well. I knew something was wrong with the first sip of the first spoonful; or I thought I knew something was wrong. But maybe lobster bisque was supposed to taste like that, revolting. So I had another sip, and then stopped. Not long after that, I started to feel ill. I couldn't face the thought of lobster. I couldn't face the thought of anything. All I could do was sit quietly and wait patiently to see whether I died or not.

I didn't die, not then anyway, but whenever I think of Julio Mariner winning the St Leger, I picture myself kneeling in front of the toilet at home and thinking, while I was being sick, 'You can do this to me, God, but I've still won £1,500.' I never have eaten lobster, though.

That good win was almost followed by another because, a few days after the St Leger, I backed Claudio Nicolai at 33–1 for the Cambridgeshire. I'd fancied Denys Smith's five year old for a long time, and I fancied him more after watching him come back from a summer break to run an unpressed trial over a trip beyond his best at Ayr. When Joe Mercer was booked for Newmarket, everything was right. By the time they started,

Claudio Nicolai was down to 10–1.

Funny course, Newmarket. Very wide but full of boxes. A furlong out, Mercer got himself stuck in a coffin. He stayed there, a winner underneath him, locked in. When time was running out, I wanted Mercer to nudge his mount sideways, and risk the stewards. It would have been worth it. It might have been all right. But he didn't.

Instead, one of the worst experiences racing has to offer. When the gap finally came, I knew it was too late, but a special act of cruelty had to be played out. Claudio Nicolai burst forward, scythed the gap down, and was beaten a neck. The next day, the headline in the *Sporting Life* read, 'Claudio Nicolai is unlucky as Baronet lasts home.' Mercer has never written to say sorry.

Early in 1979 I finished my doctoral thesis – 'The Poor Law in Bradford *c*.1834–1871: A Study of the Relief of Poverty in Mid-Nineteenth Century Bradford': 720 pages, 1,276 footnotes, an 18 page bibliography. It seemed very important at the time.

It was time to get a job. I got one at a foam rubber factory in High Wycombe. There were three of us. We had to stuff foam rubber off-cuts into a machine, clamp it closed and wait while the machine compressed them into a dense bale. Only Arnold Schwarzenegger could force enough foam rubber into the machine to flash up the 'Full' sign, and only Sylvester Stallone could clamp the door closed when the 'Full' sign had lit up. They were the two men I was working with. When I discovered that I couldn't lift the bales either, I called it a day and started the next one at Wyeth's laboratory, near Slough. I looked after the rats. At weekends, I'd bring a couple home and we'd let them run around the lounge and sit on my shoulder. They were nice rats, white ones. I liked them.

Lectureships in modern history were rare and precious things and I was lucky to be offered one at Chester College of

Higher Education. I expect it's a university now; most colleges are. Then, it was a church college, and when I saw all the tweed jackets with leather patches on the elbows, and all the students who belonged to the Christian Union, I wasn't sure I could cope with it, even with Chester racecourse nearby, so I turned the job down, and spent a year working for a sewage treatment company in Aylesbury instead.

I worked for Stan. My job was to come up with reasons why we shouldn't pay contractors the sums of money they insisted we owed them; not yet, anyway. Occasionally, it would come to a meeting. They would wheel in their team, and Stan and I would join them. Stan was big and rude and spoke with his mouth full. The meeting would start off politely. At a suitable moment, I would present an armful of figures and we would discuss them, then argue about them, then reach an impasse. Stan had one great strength. He didn't give a toss. If we could win the argument the sophisticated way, fine. If we couldn't, Stan twiddled his thumbs and looked bored and carried on eating his sandwich and, when the men in the dark suits finally stopped talking, Stan finished his sandwich and said, 'No.' Nothing else, just 'No.' When he was pressed, Stan said 'No' again, more belligerently, although he'd said it quite belligerently the first time. After that, we tried to work out whether they'd really take us to court or not.

At lunchtime, I'd walk over to the Corals shop on the far side of the town centre. When the weights came out for the 1980 Grand National, I walked over and put £20 each way on Ben Nevis at 40–1. Ben Nevis, a dual Maryland Hunt Cup winner, was a wonderful jumper of fences. Generously handicapped, he had only one Achilles heel, out of a maximum of four. He needed fast ground. For the next six weeks, I woke up every morning and hoped it wasn't raining, but it was raining; it was bucketing down. By the day of the race, I had given up hope.

Tim Forster, Ben Nevis's trainer, never had any hope in the

first place. Forster, who lives with a face like a disappointed blood-hound, is the Ambrose Bierce of racing. The author of the wonderfully bleak *Devil's Dictionary* had a jaundiced view of everything, especially if it had a person's head sitting on the top of it. ('Cabbage. A vegetable about as large and wise as a man's head.') Bierce defined an optimist as 'A proponent of the doctrine that black is white. A sufferer from an intellectual disorder that, fortunately, is not contagious.' In 1913, when he was seventy-one, Bierce crossed the United States border into Mexico to take some pictures of the revolution, and hasn't been seen since.

Like Bierce, Forster has a huge capacity for what optimists call pessimism, and pessimists call realism. He is even pessimistic about being a pessimist. 'You are either an optimist or a pessimist,' he once told me, dolefully. 'You can't do anything about it. It's the way you're born. It's much better to be an optimist, except that, if you are always expecting the worse and something good happens, then you are extra pleased.'

Whenever I think of Forster, I think of sitting with him in his battered Range Rover, watching his beloved chasers canter up the downs, telling the story of two trainers watching a bad selling hurdle together. As the field galloped by, one trainer said, 'he's by Nijinsky, you know, beautifully bred.'

'I'm beautifully bred,' said the other, 'but I'm fucking useless, too.'

One of the horses cantering up the gallop that day was being prepared for the Horse and Hound Grand Military Gold Cup at Sandown, one of the military races Forster invariably contests. I asked him why he was so keen on them. 'It's because I was qualified to ride in them myself,' he replied. 'I used to be excited about it for weeks beforehand.' Forster paused. 'It was a tremendous thrill, falling off at the first fence.'

When Ben Nevis was about to set off for the National's muddy start, Forster gave Charlie Fenwick his riding instructions. 'Keep remounting.' He didn't need to. Ben Nevis won by twenty lengths, at 40–1, the same price I'd taken weeks before. What a shrewd bet!

Unfortunately, it wasn't followed by others. I didn't back Aldaniti in 1981 (I backed Royal Mail), or Grittar in 1982 (I backed Hard Outlook), or Corbiere in 1983 (I think I may have backed something but I can't remember what it was). I did back Hallo Dandy, in 1984, after which I cultivated a rather impressive smug smile, and waited for 1985. When it arrived, I didn't back Last Suspect, followed it up by not backing West Tip, and the next year was certain that Maori Venture would fall. I still think he will.

Eventually, the National became ridiculously easy. In 1989 I backed Little Polveir at 28–1, and in 1990 did the same to Mr Frisk, at 16–1. I'd already worked out what was going to win the 1991 National. I spent the winter telling anyone prepared to listen, and some who weren't, that Seagram was the one. I told them, but I didn't do anything else about it, such as backing it. I don't know why. You know how it is, you miss the 33–1 and, while you're thinking whether you're prepared to take 25–1, it's been moved to 20–1. By the time you've finished feeling irritated about it, it's 16–1. And so it came to pass that, on the morning of the race, I still hadn't backed Seagram, and he was 12–1, which I couldn't bear to take, so I did what you do when that happens: pray that he wouldn't win. But he did win, which is why it's so difficult to believe in God.

In 1992 I had a bet the day before the National, which prevented me from having a bet the day after. The following year I backed what would have been the winner, but God was in one of his bad moods and called the race off, just to spite me. My selection in 1994 was Miinnehoma, but there was no point backing him, because the bookmaker would have claimed that I'd spelt his name wrong and refused to pay out.

After Ben Nevis had won, I got a job at Langley College, near Slough. It's called the East Berkshire College now; soon, I expect it will be called the University of East Berkshire. When I went to my room, one of the lecturers I was sharing it with was interviewing an applicant for an A-level English course. 'Do you like reading?' he asked her.

'Oh, yes,' she replied, eagerly.

'What sort of books do you like?'

'Oh, thick ones.'

At Langley, lively, questing young minds were in short supply, resulting in some bored older ones. When things got desperate, one lecturer used to say, 'Let's all join hands, and see if we can make contact with the living.'

Besides teaching, which was demanding, I carried on studying and writing. I took a two-year postgraduate diploma in management studies at Slough College (yes, it's now the Thames Valley University) for a bit of intellectual stimulation, and contributed to a joint work on 'Victorian Bradford' and to another on 'The Poor and the City'.

At least the college was only a three-minute run to the betting shop. It wasn't a characterful shop, like the ones in Cambridge and Bradford, but it had its moments. One afternoon, a woman walked in and announced in a very loud voice that she had been born in 1921 and today was her sixtieth birthday. When the manager explained that there still wasn't anything to come on her betting slip, she grabbed hold of the glass screen which separated the people who cared what had won the last at Bangor from the ones who didn't, and gave it a good shaking. We all watched, like rabbits in the headlights, as the manager tried to reason with her. While he reasoned, she shook the screen remorselessly free of its moorings. Then she raised it triumphantly above her head, and dropped it.

Afterwards, we stood around for a while, staring at the glass on the floor, and then two policemen turned up and took her away. I know exactly how she felt, as she struggled, with a total lack of success, to reach the state of grace known as being 'a good loser'. In her case, I think it was life, rather than her last computer straight forecast, that she was complaining about.

Being a good winner is easy. All you have to do is adopt an air of detached authority and explain, slowly and carefully, why only an idiot would have considered backing anything other than the winner. During the rest of the afternoon you repeat the explanation at regular intervals, pausing now and again to count your money and allow lesser punters to ask what you fancy in the next. The correct reply is, 'Nothing, that was the only horse worth backing today.' Then you smile.

Losing gracefully is a lot trickier. A good test is how you react after having a thumping great bet on a 33–1 shot which stumbles ten yards from the winning post and becomes your third photo-finish defeat in a row. If you turn to your neighbour, smile affably and say, 'It's a funny game, isn't it? That's the beauty of racing. By the way, I'm glad your 50p bet on the favourite won,' you are well on the way.

Most punters fall slightly short of that. One regular in the Ladbrokes' shop on Hall Ings, in Bradford, became so consumed by pessimism that, when he came back from the counter with his betting slip, he would deliberately drop it on the floor and stand on it. He said it saved time later. I think he may have been half a furlong short of a mile. On one occasion, he stood in the middle of the shop, flourishing his betting slip. 'See this,' he shouted. 'This is a tenner on the next favourite. And this is what it's worth.' Then he stretched his arms out in front of him, folded the slip up, folded it again, and tore it into small pieces. Then he threw them in the air. 'Help yourself, maties, because they aren't worth a thing.' The funny thing is, he was right; they weren't.

I've never been tempted to do that, but I have always preferred, when I've had a bet, to watch or listen to the race on my own. That way, you don't have someone asking what you've backed and then saying, 'He's going to win, isn't he?' forcing you to reply, 'No, he's going to get stuffed by that thing flying up the rails which hasn't been off for fourteen months.' If it's on television, there's a lot to be said for watching at home, where virtually anything is permitted with a consenting adult (yourself) in the privacy of the building society's own home. You can scream, roll on your back and kick your legs in the air, burst out crying and swear at the horse, jockey, trainer, stewards, and God; and still keep your reputation intact. What's left of it.

At eight o'clock, every Saturday morning, for about five years, we went riding, first at Snowball Farm, near Burnham, and then to the Radnage House riding school, near Stokenchurch. We rode in small jumping competitions and over the school's cross-country course and, until I became frustrated with my shortcomings and gave up, I got a lot out of it.

I've always enjoyed studying jockeys' riding styles, and trying to spot talented apprentices, and amateur riders, before other people have spotted them. Watching jockeys, and learning what distinguishes one from another, is one of the pleasures of racing. As in any sport, the best jockeys make what is difficult look easy. Until Frankie Dettori arrived, the Flat jockey I most admired was Steve Cauthen. I had admired Lester Piggott as well – there'll never be another – but my admiration for Piggott as a rider fought a battle with the knowledge that he was a God with feet of clay: tremendously brave, dedicated, a genius in a saddle, lost out of one, Piggott's worshippers confused the man and the talent. With Our Lester, acts of simple selfishness were seen as cheekie chappie. When Piggott was convicted of tax evasion, an army of inane supporters, who either hadn't read or didn't want to read the depressing evidence, rose up to protest at the injustice of imprisoning a man who was so very good at riding horses.

But no one can deny that Lester Piggott was unique. Of all the stories told about him, some true, some apocryphal, my favourite is a Brighton story. Lester was writing a column in a national newspaper – or rather, a journalist was writing it for him. It was hard work, because it was difficult to get Lester to say anything. The journalist lived near Brighton and, on a day off, he drifted along to the racecourse. Walking back to his car afterwards, he heard a familiar voice behind him. It was Lester. 'Hello, are you driving back to London? Can I have a lift?'

The journalist explained that he lived a few miles away and was going home. 'That's a pity,' said Lester. 'I've got some stuff for the column.'

The journalist took a deep breath. 'All right, then.'

They got in the car, drove down the hill and turned right on to the London Road. 'No, not that way,' said Lester, 'go down here.'

They turned left and right, through the back streets of Brighton, the hapless hack's hackles rising until, finally, Lester said, 'Stop here.'

He got out, crossed the road and went into a small shop. A few minutes later, he came back, sat down and started to lick the ice-cream he had just bought. 'They sell the best ice-cream in the country there,' he said.

It was too much for his companion. 'I don't suppose you thought to buy me one?' he said, sharply.

'Oh,' replied Lester, with a look of surprise. 'I didn't know you liked ice-cream.'

Like Piggott and Dettori, Steve Cauthen was blessed with supreme natural talent, and the self-discipline to develop it. He was also a welcome antidote to the perverse notion, popular with the British, that the best jockeys in the world are British. That opinion retains its grip today, despite the fact that in recent years the home jockeys' championship has been won by an American, a South African and an Italian.

Cauthen arrived in Britain in 1979: a fiercely precocious talent, eighteen years old, with a record an old man would have been proud of. As an apprentice of sixteen, Cauthen had twice ridden six winners in a day at New York's Aqueduct racetrack. At seventeen, he rode more winners in New York State – 433 – than anyone before or since, and became the first rider to top $6 million in earnings. The following year, 1978, Cauthen partnered Affirmed to victory in the most prestigious hat-trick of all, the US Triple Crown: the Kentucky Derby, the Preakness Stakes, and the Belmont Stakes.

In April 1979 Cauthen nudged Marquee Universal into the lead at Salisbury to make his first ride in Britain a winning one. A month later, four days after his nineteenth birthday, Cauthen won the Two Thousand Guineas on Tap On Wood. Polite, bright and articulate, Cauthen enjoyed a honeymoon period with the press, who never mentioned his name without saying what a fine ambassador he was. Then Barry Hills' yard, where Cauthen was based, was hit by a virus. The stream of winners dried up, and the kissing stopped. The press changed its tack. Cauthen was a fine young man and a promising rider, but he was an American and, like all Americans, he couldn't ride a finish. With the British, riding a powerful finish counts for a lot.

Cauthen gradually adapted his style to British racecourses, very different from the flat, left-handed dirt tracks of America, and improved his finish. In 1982 he topped 100 winners; in 1984 he won the jockeys' championship and, the following year, after joining Henry Cecil, retained the title. During the next five years, Cauthen rode eight English Classic winners, partnering horses such as Oh So Sharp and Old Vic, Reference Point and Diminuendo, Slip Anchor and Indian Skimmer.

At his peak, in the mid-1980s, no one conveyed a sense of being in control of a situation as strongly as Cauthen. To watch him when the pressures were greatest, and the margins narrowest, was to watch a man who understood the needs and the possibilities of the moment, precisely. An acknowledged master of pace, Cauthen's trade mark was dictating a race from the front, although he always insisted that he was just as happy racing off the pace.

His priority was always to keep his horse balanced, and his technique in a finish was a natural extension of the neatly poised style he adopted throughout a race.

When a horse came under pressure, some of Cauthen's contemporaries made a speedy resort to the whip. Cauthen, with more skill to draw on, selected from a wider range of aids. He clicked his tongue, changed his hands on the reins, squeezed a bit more and, only then, if he thought it would help, picked up the whip. When other jockeys raised their whips, it was a signal of impending defeat; with Cauthen, it was a sign that there was still hope. If there wasn't, he didn't use it.

In 1987, Cauthen won a titanic struggle with Pat Eddery for the jockeys' championship. Eddery was, and is, a very different rider, less pleasing to the eye. Punters love to see him go into overdrive, conjuring a winning run from his mount with a grimly powerful, not-to-be-denied, saddle-bouncing, bottom-bumping finish. Sometimes, the fireworks at the end of a race are made necessary by a tactical mistake earlier on.

At Goodwood, in August 1988, Preziosa clipped the heels of a horse in front, and fell, injuring Cauthen's neck. He was soon race-riding again, but the accident, the exhausting contest with Eddery, and a debilitating battle with his weight persuaded Cauthen to adopt a more selective approach. He had fewer rides, and focused his ambition on the top prizes. Towards the end of his career, Cauthen didn't go for the gaps with the same dare, and the fire in a finish belonged to the newly imported star, Michael Roberts, but there were still some wonderful displays of polished skill to enjoy. In his final season, riding as first jockey to Sheikh Mohammed, Cauthen's cool control was gloriously in evidence on Twist And Turn at Newmarket's Craven meeting, when his mount surrendered the lead to Young Senor in the final half-furlong of the Feilden Stakes, and Cauthen then patiently waited his moment to drive Twist And Turn back up. A week later, when Pollen Count rallied to deny Aljadeer in the Thresher Classic Trial at Sandown, race-readers had the chance to compare Cauthen and Eddery at full stretch in a finish. The comparison clearly favoured Cauthen.

But the expected flood of Group One winners failed to materialise and, at the end of the 1992 season, aged thirty-two, Cauthen retired and returned to Kentucky. Unlike Lester Piggott, Cauthen could easily imagine life without racing.

For the fourteen seasons that Cauthen was here, I enjoyed watching him enormously, and he played a part in the spreading acknowledgement that British jockeys might have something to learn from their American counterparts. We still thought Americans were weak in a finish, which was why Cash Asmussen, the darling of Paris, was never a star in Britain; but a new generation of jockeys, headed by Alan Munro, were starting to ride the US way.

As the internationalisation of racing progressed, there were some very public reminders that British riders were not necessarily the best in the world. In 1991 Mike Smith, the New York champion, won the Irish Two Thousand Guineas on Fourstars Allstar. The race exposed an embarrassing contrast between Smith, neat and balanced and close to his horse, and Christy Roche, on Star Of Gdansk, riding like a gale-rocked windmill. When I went to the 1993 Breeders' Cup at Santa Anita, in California, Jerry Bailey was asked about his shock success on Arcangues in the Breeders' Cup Classic. The Texan described how he had moved alongside a European-ridden horse. He didn't know who it was, he just knew it was a European rider. How did he know that? The Americans all sniggered. Bailey smirked. 'Well,' he replied, 'he was kinda flopping about.' Bailey was talking about Walter Swinburn, one of our most stylish riders.

Americans don't think much of British jockeys, and it is only partly because Americans can be maddeningly chauvinistic and insular and shamefully ignorant of European racing and riding requirements. Many of the best jockeys in the world are to be found in the United States: riders like Eddie Delahoussaye and Chris McCarron, Mike Smith, Gary Stevens and Kent Desormeaux. The British may admire Pat Eddery's style, but the Americans are dismissive. Brad Free, writing in the *Daily Racing Form*, America's *Sporting Life*, noted, relatively politely, 'Pat Eddery makes few style points from American racing observers. He won Breeders' Cups on Pebbles and Sheikh Albadou but his style is not conducive to the tight American way of riding.' In the States, as much attention is paid to what a jockey does in the first quarter of a race as in the last, and Eddery's relatively upright style, like that of many other European jockeys, seems clumsily inefficient. It makes no aerodynamic sense. It cannot be the best way to be in unison with the horse.

A rider like Dettori, whose style combines influences from both sides of the Atlantic, matches the best in the world on any criteria, and British jockeys are better than any other in at least one respect, their use of the whip. The top American jockeys switch whip hands with silken smoothness, but some Stateside riders, like Australian jockeys, are prone to slash away with their whips in a way that makes their mounts veer off a straight line, and become unbalanced. Britain's stricter whip rules have made today's British jockeys ride better and, as a generation, they are way ahead of those who went before.

## Chapter Seven

# You Can't Beat the System

A friend visiting W. C. Fields on his deathbed was amazed to see the lifelong cynic avidly studying the Bible. When he asked Fields what he was doing, the old sour drawled, 'Just looking for a loophole.'

Punters spend lifetimes looking for that elusive loophole. The late *Sporting Chronicle* used to publish system after system to help readers in their search for the Holy Grail. Sid James discovered the best system, in *Carry On At Your Convenience*. It involved reading out the runners until Hattie Jacques's budgerigar (or it may have been a canary) tweeted; that was the one you backed. It won Sid a fortune. Most systems don't work nearly as well, and the ones that do have a horrible habit of draining all the excitement and humour out of betting.

One day in 1992 I was standing in a betting shop, when a punter came up to me, and smirked. I knew what he was going to say, and he didn't give me a pleasant surprise by not saying it. 'Outsider of three. Never fails. Fourteen to one. Did you have it?'

'No,' I said.

Beldi had just won a three-horse race at Brighton and, in betting shops across the land, punters were turning to each other and chanting, 'Outsider of three.' The next day, the newspapers took up the chant. '14–1 Beldi proves the old adage right,' said the *Sporting Life*; 'Outsider of three does it again,' trumpeted the *Racing Post*. I thought I'd take a closer look and discovered, to my curmudgeonly satisfaction, that the hypothesis was what scientists call 'complete bollocks'.

During the 1991 Flat season, there were seventy-five races with three runners. The outsider won only three of them, with a fourth race won by a joint second and third favourite. Three and a half out of seventy-five; and the longest priced winner was 9–2. Followers of the system spent 1991 handing over £1 coins while the man on the other side of the counter kept handing back 19p. What a system. Blind followers of the favourite fared a lot better; they got back 98p in the £1.

The system was slightly less fatal over jumps because favourites and second favourites sometimes did the decent thing and keeled over. During the 1990–1 season, there were 147 races with three runners, of which seventeen were won by the outsider, with the joint second and third favourite triumphing seven times. The high spot was at Plumpton, when Mrs Ledger won on The Fruit at 14–1. Usually, the outsider started at much shorter odds: eight of the seventeen winning outsiders were returned at less than 5–2. Indiscriminate supporters of the time-honoured system lost 32p in the £1, compared with 17p if you opted for the second favourite, and less than 4p if you stuck to the favourite.

What punters should be shouting is, 'Outsider of three stuffed again. Did you have that favourite?'

There were only three systems that ever attracted me. I found the first one in a splendid little booklet called *The Psychology and System of Profitable Betting*. I don't know who wrote it, because the cover was missing, but it advertised itself as 'the

world's most powerful betting plan for gamblers'. The Pilot, as
the author called himself, likened the business of betting to the
ocean, and launched his venture with a hearty 'All aboard,
Captain, let's set sail!' Ahead of his time, The Pilot liked to
interact with his readers, and started with a question. 'Why is
betting the world's number one most perfect business?' For
those who don't know, the answer is 'Because there is no heavy
lifting, no emergency call-outs, no redundancies.' But, The
Pilot warned, 'Caution must be your watchword. Do not overdo
caning one bookmaker.' When you have given Ladbrokes a past-
ing, give them a break, and move on to Hills. And beware your
enemies. 'Who are the punter's enemies? All those who doubt
your ability to make a profit in betting, and anyone who drops
litter.'

It took a while for The Pilot to navigate his way out of the
estuary and into the open sea but, eventually, we were under
way. As he said himself, 'You must start somewhere. Do start.
You will never get anywhere until you start.' When you have
started, 'DO NOT DRINK – you are working.' The Pilot was
vague about the nature of the work – very vague – but he did
end up with an encouraging exhortation. 'Be warned,' he
warned, 'of letting greed run away with you, and be careful to
spread this technique around various bookmakers. It is a real
killer.'

Rather like my second favourite system: the one used by
Patrick Evans. In the nineteenth century an ear, nose and
throat specialist called Wilhelm Fliess reached the conclusion that all men and women were governed by 23 and 28
day rhythms, which he called biorhythms. So were plants,
such as rhubarb, and so were racehorses. According to
Evans, unfavourable biodynamics were the cause of the fractures suffered by Arkle and Mill Reef. They explained why
Roberto ran disappointingly in the 1972 Irish Derby and
Prix de l'Arc de Triomphe, and why the 1969 Two Thousand

Guineas favourite, Ribofilio, had flopped.

Vincent O'Brien was a great trainer but, when it came to biodynamics, he had a lot to learn. He sent Roberto on a suicidal mission to the Irish Derby, aged 1,204 days, without giving a thought to the fact that $1,204 = 28 \times 43$. When Roberto set off for Paris, aged 1,303 days, Evans could see disaster coming – or, at least, he saw it coming back. 'In my opinion,' wrote Evans (afterwards), 'it was a bad risk to run Roberto because his biodynamics were unfavourable. He was running on a predictable off-day.' Just how predictable you can gather from the fact that 1,303 equals 23 squared (529) plus $17 \times 18 \times 2$ (612) plus $18 \times 9$ (162). Furthermore, it equals $23 \times 42$ (966) plus 337.

Of course, it isn't always as straightforward as that: 18 and 33 are also significant numbers, and 17 is 'the key in the lock. A unique structure possessing special qualities of symmetry and economy.' This became obvious in the case of Ribofilio, whose dismal performance in the 1969 Two Thousand Guineas led to persistent but unconfirmed suspicions of doping. Not so, said Evans. On that fateful day, Ribofilio was 1,121 days old. If Fulke Johnson Houghton had taken the obvious precaution of dividing by 23, he would have discovered, to his horror, that 1,121 equals $23 \times 48$ (1,104) plus 17. Over to Evans.

'This brings us to a golden rule. Always beware the 17th day in the 23 day rhythm. I would advise backers to leave severely alone all horses running on such a day. It is a severe day off; a time when the system is so occupied with its internal affairs that it has little or no energy to spare for coping with demands from the outside world.'

I liked Evans's system, and I tested it on subsequent Classics, including the 1991 Two Thousand Guineas. The hot favourite, Marju, was clearly going to be in desperate trouble. Marju was foaled on 12 March 1988, which made him 1,148 days old on the day that mattered, 4 May 1991. How unlucky can you get?

28 × 41 = 1,148. As if that wasn't bad enough, 1,148 also equals 28 × 18 (504) plus 23 × 28 (644). Doubly damned! It was no surprise that Marju was injured during the race and finished a painfully disappointing eleventh. If Evans had been at hand to advise John Dunlop, Marju would never have run.

Nor would Bog Trotter. Even Lester Piggott's wizardry couldn't overcome the fact that Bog Trotter was 1,120 days old or, put another way, 28 × 40. No wonder he finished twelfth. It could have been worse. He could have been riding Mystiko. Guineas day was Mystiko's 1,167th birthday, and 1,167 = 23 × 50 (1,150) plus 17. You know that it is written, beware the 17th day in the 23 day rhythm. No chance.

True, Mystiko did win the Guineas, but what you've got to remember is that Evans issued a warning. 'Not all periodic days are off-days,' he reminded us, 'and not all off-days are periodic. Periodic days don't always matter. Sometimes horses run well on them.' That explains Mystiko's victory, although it does make it a bit tricky, because you don't know whether you want your horse to be off or not.

Evans tried to explain which periodic days mattered and which didn't, but it wasn't easy going. The first bit was obvious enough: '23 × 20 is congruent to 18 (mod 17). These transformations between the four symmetrically placed sub-groups in the multiplication table of Z17 provide much of the structure of biodynamics.' I think we can all agree on that, but then there is 'the famous theorem that there are 230 movement-groups (infinite discrete groups of congruent transformations) and there is also the fundamental space-lattice known as "the 14 points of Bravais".' Indeed.

Evans's system had its flaws, but it was the most interesting one I came across until I visited my first professional punter, Paul Cooper. When I visited Cooper, at his offices in Guildford, I didn't know what to expect, but I was certain of one thing. This man, who, enviably, hadn't had a proper job since he was twenty, would be selective, highly selective. Most days, most weeks, he wouldn't have a bet. There would be no 'having an interest', no chasing, no bets on half-fancies, no sentiment, no backing something because you've backed it so many times that it would hurt not to back it on the day when it does finally win. Instead, there would be analysis, mathematical calculations, talk of 'over-rounds' and standard times and weeks of waiting for a small chink of opportunity, ruthlessly exploited. Cooper would be calm, rational, detached. Not a gambler at all, really.

When I arrived, he was watching a cricket match on television. He had a bet on that, then he had a bet on the tennis, then he started on the racing. Cooper's approach to betting seemed to be as carefully targeted as a blunderbuss. He freely admitted that he bet almost every day and, during Royal Ascot, on almost every race.

What made Cooper, thirty-two when I met him, such an engaging character was his idiosyncrasy. He described himself as a form student and time student and observer of trends, above all committed to seeking out value (serious punters are always committed to seeking out value); and yet it wasn't his methods that were impressive, but his independent spirit. Cooper was intelligent, and sharp, and always impeccably dressed, but above all he was his own man, a step outside the circle. He didn't have a burning desire to make money; he had a burning desire to make his own decisions, to be different, to prove people wrong. What was interesting about him wasn't how he gambled, but why.

Cooper's biggest bet was £26,000 on Glencroft in the 1988 Bovis Handicap at Ascot. David Chapman's sprinter swerved leaving the stalls, lost at least five lengths and was beaten less than two. Never mind: at the same meeting a few years earlier, Cooper had backed twelve winners from fifteen selections and won £107,000. He claimed to have had forty-one credit accounts closed, for a different reason from the one book-makers sometimes gave me, but the red books which housed Cooper's carefully kept accounts suggested that his success was based largely on the discovery of one of those elusive loopholes.

At some racecourses, the outcome of races was strongly influenced by the positioning of the starting stalls, and which stalls different horses occupied. At Thirsk, in sprint races, horses with a high draw often had a big advantage, but it wasn't always adequately reflected in the runners' starting prices. Bookmakers had introduced a bet called a Tricast, which required you to forecast the first three home in the correct order. The dividend was based on the horses' SPs. In 1989, twenty-three runners entered the stalls for the Dick Peacock Sprint Handicap. Cooper combined the high-drawn runners, some of whom appeared to have little chance on form, in a series of Tricasts. The first three home were drawn 21, 23 and 22. Their starting prices were 20–1, 25–1 and 33–1. The Tricast paid £13,673 for a £1 stake, and Cooper brushed up against Ladbrokes' £250,000 limit. A year later, although the bookmakers were more wary, the first three home in the same race were drawn 18, 19 and 16 in a field of 16 (there were three non-runners). The horse drawn 17 finished fourth. Cooper pocketed another six-figure sum. The Thirsk Tricasts made those years. In 1989 Cooper's profit from betting on horses was £201,000; in 1990, £129,000. On the other hand, in 1984 he lost £28,000, in 1985, £11,000, and in 1986, £104,000.

During the winter, Cooper liked to disappear to America, where he could indulge his passion for large Tote pools. In the summer, I'd occasionally bump into him at Newmarket or Ascot. It was impossible to tell whether he was doing badly or well. I hoped he was doing well, because he was refreshingly different from the crowd; but, if I had to bet on it, I'd guess that eventually the people on the other side of the railings will get him, because Cooper is a player, and it's hard to be a player and a winner.

Johnny Lights was different in almost every respect. Where Cooper was slim, dapper, well educated, Lights was fat and shambolic and sounded as if he'd never been to school in his life, which he barely had. It didn't stop him living in a big house in a select private road near Epsom, paid for by gambling. Solid London, when he was fifteen Lights earned his betting money by ticket-touting and selling perfume, jewellery and umbrellas in Oxford Street. And he learnt his gambling lore the hard way, by being, as he liked to put it, 'ironed out with great regularity'. Forty-eight now, what marked him out from most punters was that he learnt from his mistakes. Clerking for a bookmaker at New Cross dogs, he watched a lot of punters lose, and a select handful win. The select few didn't have many bets.

Lights made his money by knowing those who knew. He's spent his life hovering around the bookmakers' pitches on the rails, being nosey, learning who was worth listening to, and who wasn't. Actions speak louder than words, and Lights loved the sight of knowledgeable but prudent owners betting beyond their norm.

Take Jim McAllister. In 1982, he owned a three-year-old maiden called Mr Fluorocarbon. McAllister wasn't free with his money, but Lights had received strong messages about Mr Fluorocarbon. Before the colt made his seasonal debut, at Newbury, Lights had been told that Lester Piggott had told Henry Cecil, the colt's trainer, that Mr Fluorocarbon would win the Queen Anne Stakes at Royal Ascot. He wondered if the owner had received the same encouragement. When McAllister approached a rails bookmaker, Lights was listening. He thought McAllister might have what, for him, was a big bet, say £1,000. He heard him ask for £10,000. That was the signal Lights had been waiting for. He hurried his unhurriable shape along the line, and collected £30,000.

Four years later, when the messages for debutante Forest Flower were equally strong, Lights staked £20,000 at about 7–4; but even that wasn't his biggest win. That came in 1989, when a private line to Dick Hern told Lights that the trainer of two Derby winners, Troy and Henbit, had never been as confident as he was that Nashwan would win the Blue Riband. Lights' big ears and brave pocket won him £75,000.

Where Cooper never listened to other people's advice, Lights was on a state of constant alert for signals and messages – and stewards' enquiries. When bookmakers had big liabilities on the runner-up, and there was a stewards' enquiry, they were tempted to seek insurance against a welcome loser being converted into an unwelcome winner. Generous odds were sometimes available against the winner keeping the race. Lights has made tens of thousands of pounds saying 'yes, please' to overgenerous odds on stewards' enquiries, despite Rock Hopper.

In 1991, at Royal Ascot, Rock Hopper was odds-on favourite for the Hardwicke Stakes, but was narrowly beaten by Topanoora. Pat Eddery, Rock Hopper's partner, objected on the grounds that Topanoora had taken his ground in the final furlong. Lights was convinced that nothing had happened in the last furlong to justify reversing the placings, and backed his opinion with £44,000. The stewards agreed with him, and overruled Eddery's objection; but they also decided that Rock Hopper had been the victim of interference earlier in the straight, and threw the winner out.

For a dreadful twenty-four hours, Lights lost his grip on the hardest-won lesson of all, that you mustn't chase your losses. He got the hots, tried to smash his way out, and smashed in another £56,000. No wonder Lights has a vulnerable, troubled look in his eye. He knows what it's like, and he's terrified of going skint. It's the knowledge that defeat is an edge away which saves the handful of intermittently successful professionals, like Cooper and Lights, from arrogance.

With every race televised, scrutinised, analysed by an army of experts and accountant-sharp bookmakers, racing has become a horribly challenging field of battle. Even Alex Bird, the most famous of all professional punters, who made much of his money betting on photo-finishes, came to believe that it was no longer possible to make a living backing horses. But you might make a living backing something else, in a field where an expert, however briefly, can still know more than the bookmakers. Where there might still be a loophole.

One day, I had a phone call from a Midlands bookmaker called Arthur Whitaker. Whitaker was in a bit of a state. One of his staff had offered 100–1 against anyone scoring a hole in one during the Benson and Hedges tournament at St Mellion. He had offered the same odds against the same eventuality at the Volvo PGA Championship at Wentworth, and at the British Open at Royal Birkdale. And there had been a hole in one at all three of them. The man who had asked Whitaker's acting manager for a price had put £50, tax paid, on each of the three tournaments. Whitaker was staring at betting slips worth £15,000, and wriggling. He wanted to know what the *Sporting Life* thought, because he didn't intend to pay. It was obviously a mistake by an inexperienced member of staff, who should have got the bet approved before accepting it. The punter had been to other local shops, which smacked of a conspiracy. Whitaker would pay out at the 'correct' odds.

Other small bookmakers, from Sussex to Seahouses, had made the same mistake, and during the next few days I received a string of calls from betting-shop proprietors, calling 'con'. I also received a call from Paul Simons, and arranged to meet him and his friend John Carter at a motorway service station. They told me what they had done. The idea was brilliant, and simple, although its execution was sometimes dubious.

If you ask most people what the odds are against anyone scoring a hole in one at a named golf tournament, they will say they are very long. But, strangely, they aren't very long, they are very short: as short as 6–4. In 1990, there were thirty holes in one during the thirty-eight major tournaments. Paul and John were sharp Essex lads in their mid-twenties – a bit over-sharp. They knew what the true odds against a hole in one were, and they knew that most people, even bookmakers, thought the odds were longer. The big bookmakers had learned the hard way, and by 1991 there was no longer anything to be gained from asking Ladbrokes, Hills or Corals to quote a price. So Paul and John, who had nibbled at the idea before, planned a round-Britain tour of smaller independent bookmakers.

They didn't show a great regard for the truth in their efforts to persuade bookmakers to offer healthy odds, but it wasn't a game. They were risking real money to make real money. By the time the three major tournaments which Arthur Whitaker had taken bets on were over, Simons and Carter had won £300,000. When Miguel Angel Jimenez scored an ace at the seventeenth hole in the European Open at Walton Heath on 29 August, they hit the half-million pound mark – on paper.

Winning was one thing; getting paid was another. That was partly why Simons had called me. The day they had earmarked for a repeat visit to Arthur Whitaker's was the day the *Sporting Life* reported that Whitaker didn't intend to pay. As they retraced their steps around the country, the *Life*'s reports followed them. Some bookmakers paid up; others didn't, but instead joined the queue waiting for a ruling from the newspaper's arbitration service, the Green Seal service.

They didn't have to wait long. At the end of July the *Life* declared:

Our decision is that there is a world of difference between a palpable error and an error of judgment. If a bookmaker (or member of his staff) accepts a bet at mutually agreed odds – and neither the bet nor the laying procedures contravene the bookmaker's rules – there is no way in which the bet can be retrospectively voided or amended.

It is one thing for a bookie's clerk to misread a screen display and for the price to be corrected under a 'palpable error' rule, but it is quite another for a bookmaker – who has adjudged that a bet represents a reasonable risk and accepted the business – to attempt to change the terms when his naïvety or generosity becomes apparent.

Unless a bookmaker who has laid over-generous odds about a hole-in-one has a clear and unambiguous rule giving him the right to void or amend the bet for good reason, he has no option except to pay up.

Whitaker waited for a ruling on his specific case, and then paid up. Most other bookmakers followed suit and, in the end, Paul and John collected all but about £80,000 of their £500,000 winnings. Most of the £80,000 was owed by bookmakers who closed down. The 'Hole-In-One Gang' published a racy little book, with that title, and I occasionally see Paul at a southern race meeting, looking intent, and walking quickly, seeking out another loophole.

They were the biggest winners I have known. I'm not sure who the biggest loser was, but I know who was the worst loser. Philip Tilson didn't find a loophole, he fell down one.

On Derby Day 1993, the student son of a Nottinghamshire publican walked into Ladbrokes' betting shop in Mansfield Woodhouse and wrote out a £1 Tricast bet for the Derby. Tilson forecast that Commander In Chief would be first, at 7–1, Blue Judge second, at 150–1, and Blues Traveller third, also at 150–1. Then he added a 50p Tricast combination, covering the same three horses, in any order. He needn't have bothered, because he had been right the first time. It was the sort of bet that comes up only once in several reincarnations.

There was one small snag. Ladbrokes weren't offering Tricast bets on the Derby. The bet had been accepted in error. If Tilson had walked into a William Hill shop and placed the same bet, he would have won £116,400, but it wasn't one of Hill's shops, it was one of Ladbrokes'. And Ladbrokes' 'Fair Play' rules stated that 'Any Tricasts accepted for races which we have not specified will be settled as Computer Straight Forecasts on the selections nominated to finish first and second, with the selection nominated for third place discounted.' Tilson was entitled to £728.64.

While the *Sporting Life*'s Green Seal service pondered the case, I tried to persuade Ladbrokes that a more equitable approach would be to settle the bet as a Trio, a bet which was available on the Derby, and was closest in intent to a Tricast. Both required the punter to select the first three home, the Tricast in the correct order, the Trio in any order. The Green Seal service ruled that Ladbrokes were technically correct, but suggested an ex-gratia payment based on the Trio dividend of £16,935 to a £1 stake. Ladbrokes agreed, and offered Tilson £33,870, equal to two winning Trios.

I phoned Tilson with the good news, expecting him to be, if not gruntled, then not disgruntled. Tilson wasn't exactly disgruntled, but he wasn't gruntled, either. 'It's better than they were offering me at first,' he told me, flatly, 'but it's not exactly what I had hoped.'

Trying to jolly him along a bit, I said, 'I know thirty-four grand isn't as good as a hundred and sixteen grand, but it's a lot better than £728, which is what they were going to give you.'

Tilson was no more impressed than he had been to start with, and I wasn't very surprised when, the next day, he told me that he had decided to turn down Ladbrokes' offer, and appeal to the Tattersalls Committee, the ultimate arbiter of betting disputes. I, and others, tried hard to dissuade him. I warned Tilson that he would almost certainly lose the case, because Tattersalls were likely to rule that Ladbrokes had settled the bet in accordance with their rules. The rules weren't fair, but they were the advertised rules, and Ladbrokes were entitled to insist that the bet be settled under them. The offer of £33,870 was the best he would get. If he insisted on going to Tattersalls, there was a serious danger that he would be awarded £728.64, and have to pay £400 for the privilege of having his case heard.

But Tilson wouldn't be persuaded. As far as he was concerned, Ladbrokes had accepted his bet, and they should honour it, full stop. If Tattersalls Committee let him down, he would take Ladbrokes to court. I told him that was a nonstarter, but he wasn't listening.

I expected the worst, and was over-optimistic. Tilson had told me that he was eighteen, the minimum age for admission to a betting shop. Ladbrokes discovered that he was only seventeen. After taking legal advice, Tattersalls Committee decided that they could still issue a ruling. They ruled that the bet should be settled as a Computer Straight Forecast, under Ladbrokes' rules. Tilson should be paid £728.64. Ladbrokes also took legal advice, and then announced that they had no option but to declare the bet void, and return Tilson's stake – £4.40.

When I spoke to him afterwards, Tilson still wasn't prepared to admit that it might have been a good idea to have accepted the £33,870, in which case the issue of his age would never have arisen. Philip Tilson: the man who turned down £33,870 in favour of losing £400. And I thought I was stupid.

But we haven't yet got round to the only other system that attracted me. To tell you about it, I'd better change some of the facts; the principle isn't affected.

Nowadays, you can bet on what the aggregate winning

distance will be at a particular race meeting. One day, I casually looked at the card, and casually looked at Sporting Index's quote for aggregate winning distances. Let's say it was 38–41. That is, Sporting Index's prediction was that, if you added up the winning distances for all six races, the total would be between 38 and 41 lengths. If you thought it would be less than 38, you 'sold' at 38, for so much per length; if you thought the total would come to more than 41 lengths, you 'bought' at 41. The more right you were, the more you won; the more wrong you were, the more you lost. Sporting Index's quote was updated after each race. If things had gone your way, you could get out at a profit; if they hadn't, you could get out at a loss, or hang in there, and see what happened next.

One day, I watched a particular race. It was a small field, with a justifiably hot favourite. The favourite could have won by a long way, but the jockey chose to win by a relatively small margin. It made me think. When calculating their quote of 38–41, Sporting Index would have allowed many lengths for that particular race. If you had 'sold' the winning lengths, you could have 'closed' your bet after the race and made a healthy profit, at much longer odds than the price of the favourite. But that was with hindsight. How could you know that the jockey would choose to win by, let us say, two lengths, when he could easily have won by twenty? I couldn't know, but the trainer and jockey might know.

As it happened, I knew the trainer quite well. That evening, I rang him, and pointed out that, barring accidents, the short-priced winner could have been turned into a longer priced winner, with no rules broken. At that time, very few trainers knew what spread betting was, but the one I phoned knew. He had made a nice profit that day.

I still look at some races, especially over jumps, and wonder if the finish has been shaped by a spread bet. The rider of the comfortable winner eases down heavily, or pushes out vigorously, for no obvious reason; the rider of the runner-up, with no prospect of catching the winner, or of being caught for second place, rides his mount out strongly to the line.

Why? I wonder why.

# Chapter Eight

# Ragbag

I suppose I can blame what happened in 1987 on what happened in 1986. I can only remember three things about 1986.

The first was going to Kempton one Thursday in July with my head full of Harbour Bazaar. I thought about him before breakfast, during breakfast, and after breakfast. I thought about him in the car to Kempton and when I was at Kempton. I kept looking at my watch to see how much longer I would have to wait for the first show of betting for the 4.15 from Yarmouth, where Harbour Bazaar was running in an eight-runner maiden race. I paced between the stands and the betting shop beneath the stands. I watched a race from Kempton, listened to a commentary from Yarmouth, had another cup of tea, and wished that it was ten past four; and, eventually, it was.

Predictably, Waajib was the 11–4 on favourite, but Harbour Bazaar was the best each-way steal I had seen for a long time. He was a near-certainty to finish third, at 20–1. In a race like that, on a horse like that, the Tote place dividend is always dreadful. It is better to back the horse each way with a

121

bookmaker, if they will let you, and write off the win stake. So that is what I did.

Harbour Bazaar duly finished third, comfortably clear of the rest of the field. I scribbled a figure on the back of my ticket and waited for them to weigh in. While I was waiting, an announcement arrived. 'Objection at Yarmouth . . . The clerk of the scales objects to the third.' When the clerk of the scales lodges an objection, there can be only one outcome. There was. Jimmy Carter, Harbour Bazaar's jockey, had forgotten to weigh in.

The second thing I remember is being at Newbury, one September Saturday, watching television in the bar under the stand. As I watched, the runners were going down for the 2.10 at Ayr. That prompted me to look at the form and, if you look at the form long enough, eventually you fancy something. I looked at it long enough to fancy Emerald Eagle, at 8–1. It was quite a long way from the bar to the racecourse betting shop, but I sprinted over and scrawled out a betting slip. Then I ran back to the bar with the television in it. They were off, and so was Emerald Eagle. As he passed the winning post, two and a half lengths in front of the others, I savoured the warm glow of relief which engulfed me. Later, I strolled back to the betting shop and, with a professional's detached air, handed over my ticket for admiration. The lady behind the counter informed me that, when I placed my bet, they were already off, but she was prepared to give me my money back.

The other thing that happened in 1986 happened in December. There was a novice chase at Fontwell which was so awful that John Bosley's Fada had as good a chance as anything else did of winning it. I was cashless in Esher, but that didn't matter because I could ring Vic, the Wooburn Green bookie who lives in a very big house with a door bell that plays a bit of Mahler's Seventh Symphony every time you turn up to give him a cheque. So I found a telephone kiosk, went into it, and was just about to say, 'Twenty pounds each-way Fada,' when the door opened. I recognised who it was immediately. It was my wife.

Suddenly, 'Twenty pounds each-way Fada' didn't seem the right thing to say, so I didn't say it. For a while, I didn't say anything. I waited for my mouth to re-establish contact with my brain. It took so long, I began to wonder whether it ever would.

While I waited, Lesley asked impatiently, 'What are you doing?' It was a reasonable question to ask, but a difficult one to answer. I was waiting for a hand to work its way along the telephone wire and drag me back up it. I was waiting to have a coronary so that she would feel sorry for me. Neither happened.

It must have been 10,000–1 against Lesley turning up at that telephone kiosk, which was a lot longer odds than Fada. Fada was only 20–1. On the other hand, he did win by thirty lengths.

Maybe that's why, the following year, I launched a tipping service. In the long list of embarrassing experiences life has been generous enough to provide, this ranks highly. Like placing the barrel of a gun between your teeth and pulling the trigger, it should not be attempted more than once. The main requirements, apart from desperation, greed and arrogance, are an abnormally thick skin and an inadequately developed sense of guilt, both of which I lacked. It also helps if you can pick the occasional winner.

I advertised myself as the best-qualified tipster respondents were ever likely to respond to, backing up the claim with my BA, MA (Cantab), PhD, DMS (Distinction). If I had been answering questions on the nineteenth-century poor law in Bradford, or work attitudes among lecturers at Langley College, it would have been all right; but, unfortunately, I wasn't, and it wasn't.

A single small advertisement in The *Sporting Life* produced

250 requests for a set of free details. These were rather impressive, given that they had been typed on an ancient portable typewriter. They pointed out that a £1 level stake placed indiscriminately on the mounts of the top twelve professional jockeys during the 1986 Flat season produced a pre-tax loss of £1,242, whereas the same sum staked equally indiscriminately on the mounts of the top twelve amateur riders would have produced a profit of £52. Clinchingly, I revealed that 'Just one of the twelve leading professionals returned a profit to a level stake; eight of the top twelve amateurs did so, including the top six riders.'

There were good reasons for this, which I explained with great patience and conviction, before inviting my readers to send anything from £20 to £100 for the dubious privilege of sharing my selections for part or all of the coming Flat season. 'I am perfectly satisfied that these fees are extremely modest,' I concluded, 'and I expect them to be substantially higher for new clients next season.' Having convinced myself, I was not surprised when, during the next fortnight, over £1,000 appeared through the letterbox, including subscriptions from lords and wealthy commoners.

Everything went smoothly until the time came to divulge my first selection, soon to be followed by my second and third selections. Clients were given a number and invited to phone during the day of the race. This could be difficult, particularly when I was supposed to be lecturing on the problems of the coal industry between the wars at the precise moment when Tim Thomson Jones and Geraldine Rees were being led into the stalls for the start of the Redcar Amateurs Handicap. A couple of fellow lecturers helped me out, but they couldn't help with the selections, which started slowly, and then faded. The high spot was when one client (tipsters always call them clients), phoned to congratulate me on tipping a 33–1 runner-up. He had misheard me; I had tipped something else.

Remarkably quickly, I was overcome by embarrassment. In the absence of a large, welcoming hole in the kitchen floor, next to the telephone, all I wanted to do was give people their money back. At least I showed confidence in my own selections. In fact, my clients were remarkably tolerant. They gradually stopped phoning, and didn't enquire about the terms for renewing their subscriptions, but they weren't nasty about it; a couple of fairly gentlemanly queries about one or two of my selections was the worst I got.

The final straw, although another straw wasn't needed, came in an envelope from one of my clients. He wrote to ask if I would like to subscribe to a tipping service he was about to launch. I declined and, instead, produced a set of economics worksheets for economics lecturers and wrote a booklet on *How To Stop Gambling*. The worksheets sold quite well, at £15 a set plus £2 postage and packing, but the booklets on *How To Stop Gambling* weren't as successful. I've still got a small pile of them, although I threw out a much bigger pile. I think they're quite good. I might buy one.

I had become interested in academic studies of gambling and, after devouring the literature, eventually wrote an article for the *Guardian* on 'The Problem Punters'. It bemoaned the government's failure to respond to calls for more data on the incidence of excessive gambling, and highlighted the paucity of help available to problem gamblers and their families. Shortly afterwards, I attended a workshop on adolescent gambling at Exeter University, where the author of one of the best books on the subject, Jim Orford, was based. Orford's *Excessive Appetites: A Psychological View of Addictions*, highlighted some interesting parallels between the causes, course and consequences of a range of addictive behaviours, including gambling, drinking and drug-taking. It prompted me to join the Society for the Study of Gambling, whose twice-yearly meetings, invariably interesting, I still enjoy attending. They are held in Tavistock Square. You can go to the morning session, discuss the state of bingo over lunch, give the afternoon talk on fruit-machine players in Birmingham a miss, and pop round the corner to Ladbrokes.

Advertising a tipping service produced an enthusiastic response; advertising *How To Stop Gambling: A Practical Programme* yielded a single reply from a gentleman in Paisley.

'Dear Sir,' he wrote, 'I would like to stop gambling very quickly. Could you give me information how to go about this and how much it will cost me?'

There was a valuable lesson to be learnt. Punters want to punt, not to give up punting. I was just the same. I didn't give up, either – although I could have done, if I'd heeded *How To Stop Gambling. A Practical Programme* by Dr David Ashforth.

In those days, after we'd been racing, win or lose, broke or flush, Ian and I would often end up in El Greco's. As soon as we walked in, clutching the evening paper, Michael or Paul or George would stride up with a big smile and make a fuss of us. Paul would put a plate of olives on the table and George would bring a bottle of wine and tell us that the kleftiko was really good today, and ask how our luck was. We'd tell him, and ask how their luck was, and Paul would explain how close he'd been to getting a treble up, or a dual forecast, and Michael would whisper about his plans to sell football coupons in Cyprus, and George would tell us an amazing story about his latest trip to the casino, when he'd either won several thousand pounds or lost several thousand pounds, or possibly both. When he'd gone to the kitchen, we'd tell each other we didn't believe a word, eat a few olives, some of them black, talk about the day's racing, and then talk about the next day's.

When all the olives were gone, and most of the wine, George would come over and talk Ian into singing with the guitarist who sat in front of the bar. He'd get a big round of applause for

'Wooden Heart' and 'The Moon's a Balloon', and then George or Paul would ask what we fancied tomorrow. Taking our responsibility seriously, we'd tell him and, the next evening, hope they hadn't taken any notice.

After that, we'd set off for the Victoria Sporting Club, or The Sportsman, or the Golden Nugget, or Charlie Chester's, and play blackjack.

Blackjack is an interesting game. On one side of the table is the dealer. She's twenty-three, comes from Romford, and looks as if she hasn't been so bored since she was forced to go to school. It's only evens about her producing a pot of strawberry jam, spreading it on the next two cards, and eating them. On the other side is a man who has drunk too much and thinks the dealer likes him. He thinks she's smiling at him in a special way, finds him very amusing, and would like to go to bed with him. He leers at her with what he thinks is an engaging smile.

Ian and I played blackjack quite well. Not very well, not *Million Dollar Blackjack* by Ken Uston well, but better than most of the players at the Victoria Sporting and other clubs, many of whom were unbelievably bad. Holding fifteen against a picture, they stand. With fourteen against a nine, they stand, although, if the same happens on the next deal, they take a card. Sometimes you want to ask why, but it's best not to. They stand because they are frightened of going bust. They think that, if they make sure they don't go bust, they have a better chance of winning than if they risk going bust. If you have fifteen against a picture, and take a card, you sometimes get a dirty look; and if you have sixteen against a picture, and take a card, which is what you should do, you get several dirty looks.

Ian sometimes played roulette, as well, but I only ever played blackjack. In roulette, the casino's advantage is too open to view, fixed and formal. It is there in blackjack, as well, but politely hidden away; and the very best players, playing under the right conditions, can exploit moments when the house temporarily loses its advantage. Some clever professionals, sophisticated computer analysts and card counters, have done just that, and been banned from every major casino in the world for their trouble – the ultimate accolade, along with forcing a change in the rules.

I have never been banned, not even from a tiny casino, not even that one in Southsea where Ian and I once walked out with more than we'd walked in with. They have never changed the rules for me, which is a pity, because I don't see how I can possibly win unless they do.

At blackjack, over a period of time, good players can expect to do better, or less badly, than bad ones. You can employ knowledge to influence the outcome, as well as enjoying the uncertainty and suspense. Roulette has suspense, too, but always looked to me like a game where the best players in the world could not escape from the table's relentless, repetitive arithmetic. If you were backing single numbers, instead of spreading your chips around and playing spin after spin, you might just as well put the whole lot on one number, one spin. That way, it leaves the rest of the evening free.

That is what a lot of us should do with the horses. It would leave the rest of life free to do what we've always promised ourselves we'd do – read all those Penguin Classics, say. When someone asks, 'Have you read *The Adventures of Ferdinand Count Fathom*, by Tobias Smollett?' I want to be able to say, 'Yes, but I preferred *The Expedition of Humphrey Clinker*'.

Later, I discovered that I was mistaken, not about Smollett, but about roulette. I met a team who had made, not a fortune, but tens of thousands of pounds playing roulette. They did it by watching the way the wheel was spun; where the ball was placed to start with, and where it ended up; the rhythm of the spinner. If the ball was more likely to end up in one section of the wheel than another, it was possible to make money. They got banned, too.

Ian and I didn't get banned but, one glorious three o'clock in the morning, we walked towards the exit of Charlie Chester's with the £400 we had just won in our pockets. When we got there, it was raining, monsooning. We didn't have an umbrella; we didn't have raincoats. So we did the obvious thing, and went back in. And half an hour later . . .

But on the whole we played sensibly. We always stopped when we hadn't got any money left.

By 1988 I was bored with teaching, and joined the National Foundation for Educational Research as a senior research officer. I spent the next sixteen months conducting a government-sponsored study into the use of the records of achievement which school-leavers in some local authorities were leaving school with. We wanted to find out what use employers, YTS managing agents, college admission tutors and careers officers were making of these documents, and what school-leavers thought of them.

I enjoyed it, although my main memory of the project is visiting a Coral's shop in Bury St Edmunds one milestone day in February 1988. It was a special shop, because it was one of the ones which had the new SIS service; the first time I had seen it. Televised racing from Taunton and Leicester, plus the dogs from Hackney and Crayford. At least, they said it was from Hackney and Crayford, and we believed them. It's difficult to tell with greyhound racing, because the cameras never show the crowd, mainly because they've never managed to find it. I don't think some of the tracks exist. Is there really somewhere called Monmore, or is it Romford with the signs changed?

Anyway, SIS meant that there was no more folding my betting slip in two, marking off the furlongs along the top edge, and following a horse's progress from the Extel man's commentary. No more living in hope that he might yet say, 'and finishing fast . . .' It was the beginning of the end of betting shops as I knew them, with a boardman and banter and long discussions about why a stewards' enquiry had been called and who had done what, all conducted from the safety of perfect ignorance.

'Went across him, didn't he, silly sod? Eddery was coming late, wasn't he?'

'What about that favourite? Never mentioned. Stewards must be blind. Bent as a nine-bob-bit, Hide, isn't he? They all are. Well, it's right, isn't it?'

'It's all bent, isn't it? Course it is. Got to be, hasn't it? They don't run it for you and me, do they? Course they don't.'

There was always one man, clutching the only working biro in the shop, who would walk across to the *Sporting Life* on the wall, the one you were looking at, and stab the Kelso card with the biro. He'd put a big hole next to number 1 in the 3.15, which was his selection, and another big hole next to number 4, which had just won, or a line which became a big hole right the way through number 7, which was the favourite he'd backed but which hadn't won.

If it had won, he'd have been at the counter for his winnings before the settler had had a chance to settle. There was always someone in front of you in the queue, who pushed a handful of betting slips under the glass screen and said, 'Anything to come on these, love?'

The sole cashier rummaged through her own stack of slips, held together by an elastic band. 'You've got £1.27 on that one, Joe.'

'Is that all? I thought it was more than that,' says Joe, as another punter joins the queue.

'I'll check for you,' she replies. 'No, that's right. You've just got that one place.'

Joe points one of his grubby fingers at one of the horses' names. 'I thought that one was placed, too,' he says.

'I don't think so, Joe, I'll just check for you. No, it's right, Joe. He came last of twenty-eight.'

'Did he? And I thought he was placed.'

Then they move on to the next slip, while you stand, shifting from one foot to the other, anxiously checking on where the runners for the next at Pontefract have got to, because you want to back Mick Easterby's 10–1 shot, the one who takes up the running just as Joe says, 'So it's £1.27, then? Funny game, isn't it?'

You screw your betting slip up and drop it on the floor and turn round to find that a big fat woman has sat down where you were sitting. She rearranges her shopping bags, and breathes out heavily. 'Ooh, that's better. My feet are killing me. You've dropped your ticket, love.'

'There's nothing on it.'

'Isn't there? Silly, betting, isn't it? But it's nice in here. Come and look at this cabbage.'

'Here, look at this.' Someone you've been trying not to talk to ever since he backed the winner of the first and you didn't pushes a betting slip in front of your chest. It's a £2 win double. The first leg won at 7–1 and the second leg didn't, at 4–1.

'Bad luck,' you say, because you think that's what he wants you to say. He nudges your arm. You've encouraged him.

'Here, look at this.' He pulls out another slip. It's another £2 win double. The first leg lost at 6–4 and the second leg won at 8–1.

'Bad luck.' He squeezes your arm. 'Here, look at this.'

The woman's still in your seat, showing off her cabbage, and the man who always sits in the seat in the corner is still sitting there. It's his seat; he doesn't like to leave it. Sometimes he has to leave it, to place a bet, to collect his winnings, to go to the toilet. When that happens, he leaves his *Sporting Life* on the seat, and his biro and betting slips on the shelf above, and a bag next to the legs which hold the stool up.

'That's my seat, mate. Look, there's my trousers.'

So you wander across to have a look at the board, and get caught again. 'Did you have that?'

'No.'

'Didn't you? Best bet of the day. I've been waiting for it for three weeks. Should have had more than fifty on it, really. Couldn't be beaten, could it? What did you do?'

You tell him. 'You didn't? Pity you didn't tell me. I could have put you straight. You'd have saved your money. Lose much?'

'£20.'

'Did you? Not too bad, then. I won £700. Should have been more, really. Anyway, must be going. Better luck next time, although I don't believe in luck. Tara.'

As he walks out, she walks in. She glides across to a tall stool, raises herself on to it, and crosses her long, bare legs. Her short skirt clings to her narrow hips. She smiles directly at you; a full, open-mouthed, lipsticked smile. Then she sits up straight and draws her shoulders back. 'I've never been here before,' she whispers. 'I wonder if you could help me.'

Well, the other bits were true.

That August, we went on holiday to Devon for a few days. I was full of excitement, could hardly wait to get Wednesday's *Sporting Life*. The worst thing about holidays was that you didn't know where your next *Sporting Life* was coming from, or your next betting shop, or even your next telephone kiosk. In the space of a three-hour drive, all life's most important certainties had vanished – the newsagent on the Green, VJ Racing opposite, the telephone kiosk in Flackwell Heath, just along from Skyport Pools. It was horrible.

I had to get Wednesday's *Sporting Life*, because the first piece I wrote for them was going to be in it. I was nervous and excited and impatient to see it. And there it was, at the top of page 5 – 'David Ashworth takes a look at some equine enigmas and eccentrics.' I was hoping it would be David Ashforth, but it was someone very like him. There was a picture of Ile De Chypre, who had given me the idea in the first place, and four pictures showing Jellaby putting his foot in a hole and falling over when he had the 1978 Lockinge Stakes at Newbury at his mercy.

When I went back to work, I proudly showed the piece to a colleague called Rosemary. Although David, another colleague, could do a brilliant impersonation of Brian Clough, most researchers had higher things on their minds than Ile De Chypre unseating Greville Starkey in the King George V Handicap at Ascot. There was very little demand for the *Life* in the NFER library. After a couple of weeks, I asked Rosemary if she had finished with my article. She seemed to have mislaid it. She knew she had taken it home, but couldn't remember what she had done with it. A few days later, it turned up, crumpled and dirty. 'I'm sorry,' she said. 'It was on the floor of the rabbit hutch.'

It's important to keep horse racing in perspective.

For the next two years, I combined my full-time job at the NFER with writing features and other racing-related articles, mainly for the *Sporting Life*. Alastair Down, then the *Life*'s larger-than-life features editor, now the *Life*'s larger-than-life associate editor, would leave a telephone message for me with the NFER's ancient and idiosyncratic receptionist. Later, we would discuss the fact that the message hadn't arrived. I would wander down to reception, and ask the receptionist if she had taken a message for me. 'I think there was something,' she would say, picking up the wastepaper bin, prior to rummaging around in it. 'Here it is,' triumphantly. 'I thought I'd got it somewhere. Now then, what was it he said?' Racing papers weren't taken terribly seriously.

Except by me. Suddenly, I had the chance to ask the questions I wanted to ask of all those names on a page, faces at a racecourse, pictures on a television screen. In the flesh, some shrank, while others grew larger. I met trainers and jockeys and owners whom I had watched from a distance for twenty years. I didn't particularly want to meet the champions, Pat Eddery and Willie Carson, Henry Cecil and Michael Stoute; I wanted to find out what people like Sir Mark Prescott and John Matthias, Alan Bond and Ian Johnson, Bill Wightman, Paul Mellon and Brian Procter were like. They were what racing meant to me.

And I wanted to meet my early heroes. So, one day, I drove past the obelisk in Eaton Park and on to the Lodge. An old companion, short and tweeded, nervous but affable, led me through a narrow corridor into the living room where the Duchess was waiting, slightly shy and wary, smoking a ciga-rette in a long, black holder. We ate salmon for lunch, from the Duchess's estate in Scotland, where there is a mountain called Arkle. On the walls of the dining room hung paintings of the first Duke of Westminster's four Derby winners; Bend Or, Shotover, Ormonde and Flying Fox. In the centre of the dining table stood the trophy that goes to the winner of the Grand National. It was there because, in 1985, Last Suspect swished his eccentric tail and galloped up the run in at Aintree like a man on death row who has spotted an open door.

On a small side table, tucked away against a wall, were four Gold Cups. The last of them arrived in 1975, after Ten Up had brought back memories of the first three. The first three bore the dates 1964, 1965 and 1966, and all carried the inscrip-tion, 'Arkle'.

Arkle had died many years before, in 1970, yet his presence lingered on powerfully in the rooms and narrow passages of Eaton Lodge. He was in the paintings and photographs that looked out from every wall, in the horseshoes and picture books, and in his owner's memory and conversation. Anne, Duchess of Westminster, had a habit of breaking, without warning, into a broad smile. She did it while recalling the time when letters arrived addressed, 'Arkle, Westminster Abbey', or

134

'Mrs Arkle'. 'I didn't mind,' she told me, 'I was proud and honoured.'

Only a horse, but more to the Duchess. She loved Arkle; not for the times she shared with everybody on the racecourse, but for the times at home shown in the photographs, when Arkle lay in the paddock with his head on the Duchess's lap. At home, Arkle was inquisitive and placid, friendly. It was on the racecourse that there was authority, self-assurance, conceit.

Jimmy Uttley had a reputation for being conceited, too; cocky, too cocky, I had been told. Not any more. Persian War retired in 1973; Uttley the year after. Disillusioned with racing, Persian War's jockey didn't visit a racecourse again. Plagued by drink problems, he lost virtually everything. When I visited him, in 1991, he was living the quietest of lives in a small flat in Newmarket, taking things carefully, a day at a time. There were no pictures of Persian War's Champion Hurdle victories on the walls – they had gone along with everything else – but he was through the bad drinking times, and content. Chastened, quiet, a hard-won peace.

It was fifteen years since Uttley had talked about the glorious Cheltenham days. Meeting him was a privilege. It was a strange, exciting feeling, knocking on his door, twenty years later, wondering what he would look like, be like, trying to think back. His glasses made him look bookish, and a cheeky smile often broke through. After we'd talked, we went for a bit of lunch at a pub. Jimmy drank mineral water, and told me a story about a well-known Irish jockey of his day. The jockey had had a big bet on his own horse, but when they reached the final hurdle, Jimmy's mount had him beaten. As Uttley kicked into the flight, he heard an Irish voice screaming behind him, 'I've backed mine, Jimmy. For God's sake, jump off.' But Jimmy couldn't bring himself to.

John Banks, who claimed to have lost £80,000 when Persian War won his third Champion Hurdle, in 1970, had gone quiet, too.

Banks had plenty of admirers, and plenty of enemies, and in 1978, the enemies had their day. On 4 March, at Newbury, the unfortunately named Stopped won the Clarke and Smith Handicap Hurdle by an easy six lengths. A week later, Fred Winter's six-year-old ran in the William Hill Imperial Cup at Sandown, sent off 9–4 favourite but finishing only third of fifteen after being hampered at the bottom bend. The stewards summoned John Francome, the former and future champion jockey, to an enquiry and cautioned him for 'riding an ill-judged race'.

A month later, Banks was questioned by Peter Smiles, the director of Racecourse Security Services, and by Bob Anderson, its chief investigating officer. Banks admitted that he frequently phoned Francome and that Francome sometimes offered his opinion about the current form of Winter's horses. He admitted that Francome had offered an opinion on Stopped's form but denied that he had profited from it or that he gave favours in return for information. He had offered to put a couple of horses in training with Francome if he ever set up as a trainer, but denied that this was a quid pro quo for information. A few days later, it was announced that Francome and Banks were to face a Jockey Club enquiry into allegations of bribery and corruption.

Immediately before what the *Sporting Life* called 'the most sensational enquiry in the history of modern racing', Banks managed a characteristic quip. 'I hope it's over early,' he said, 'because I have a strong fancy for one in the first.' In private, he was less ebullient. He told John McCririck, 'I know some of the press, bookmakers and others wouldn't spit on me if I was on fire. Tomorrow, they will be like vultures hovering over Portman Square. They all want to peck at the carcass of John Banks.'

After a ten-hour hearing, Banks and Francome were found guilty of 'conduct likely to cause serious damage to the interests of horse racing'. Both were deemed to have breached Rule

220(ii), 'in that Francome supplied confidential information to Banks at his request concerning horses in training'. Banks was also found to have broken Rule 201(iv), in that he 'surreptitiously obtained information about a trial'. But both men were cleared of all other charges, including conspiring to do a corrupt act, and Francome was cleared of the charge of receiving presents in connection with any race other than from the owner.

The sentences were harsh. Banks was warned off for three years and fined £2,500; Francome was suspended from riding until the end of the jumps season and fined £750.

After the hearing, Francome told the waiting journalists, 'I don't believe I have done anything wrong. I have never had any monetary favours and my riding was never questioned.'

Visibly taken aback by the verdict, and the severity of the penalty, Banks complained, 'I am shocked by the decision. It was absolutely farcical. In law, the case would never even have got to court.

'I have been terribly wronged. The facts proved my pre-enquiry confidence to have been entirely justified, but I have not been judged on them. Instead, they have condemned me on my reputation and rumour.' High Court action came to nothing and it was 1981 before Banks was allowed on a racecourse again.

The man who used to drive to the racecourse in a yellow Rolls-Royce still bets on the rails. If you walk down the line you will see a purple and white sign proclaiming 'The John Banks Organisation'. If it is a big southern meeting, you may spot a short, comfortable man with heavy dark-rimmed glasses and what was once a famous black fedora hat. But the man in the fedora is quiet now. The Stopped case destroyed Banks's appetite for publicity. When I wrote to him, he sent a courteous note back: 'I am afraid my days of giving interviews are now past.'

Jeffrey Bernard, on the other hand, was perfectly prepared to give an interview, but only after he had downed the four large vodkas needed to establish contact with the outside world. Bernard had spent most of his life taking on Joe Coral in various West End betting shops and the world's supply of vodka in the Coach and Horses in Greek Street. He had lost heavily on both fronts, and some day the *Guinness Book of Records* will be invited to examine Bernard's liver before it is finally given a well-earned rest on the wall of a doctor's waiting room, 'pour décourager les autres'.

When I went to see him in Norman Balon's Soho pub, Bernard was delighted. He was delighted with *Jeffrey Bernard is Unwell* at the Apollo Theatre; delighted with Peter O'Toole, who was playing the lead with his usual long arms; delighted with the royalties, and delighted with the increased fees he could now command. Sitting on his well-worn bar stool, discarding written offers from attractive women who sent photographs of themselves for his consideration, Bernard mulled over the wonder of having just been offered £2,000 to write 350 words about a pub; not a testing subject for him. We worked out that this was over £5 a word, which is the same as £5 a letter, if you stick to words like 'a'.

I went to see the play, which was very good, although I was in the upper circle and couldn't hear all the words. If I'd known how long it was going to run for, I'd have waited for my next winner and got a seat in the stalls. The highlight was O'Toole's execution of a trick involving an egg (I think it was a brown one), a shoe (black), a biscuit tin lid (Peak Frean), and a beer glass (pint, with handle and water).

At one point, Bernard says, sagely, to Fred Winter, 'Your horses look healthy.'

'Yes,' replies Fred, 'they don't stay up all night playing cards and drinking vodka.'

I found myself developing a soft spot for the abusive Muriel Belcher. Approached by a bearded friend at a loss to know what

138

to wear to a fancy dress party, she advises him, 'Put some talc on your chin and go as an armpit.'

The only important thing the script left out was the short letter Bernard once received from Miles Kington, when Kington was literary editor of *Punch*. It read, simply: 'Are you going to do the fucking article or aren't you?' Actually, I can't remember whether the script left it out or not, but I think it's funny, so I'm putting it in.

I soon discovered that horse racing, for better and worse, was a world away from academic life. Not many trainers or jockeys would flourish on a university campus; on the other hand, not many academics have had a winner at Cheltenham.

One of the first trainers I interviewed admitted that he was so engrossed in horse racing that there was nothing else he could talk about. On the rare occasions when he was compelled to enter non-racing company, he used to buy a copy of *The Times* and prepare himself for the ordeal by plodding through the first few pages. It didn't matter because, as luck would have it, it was racing I wanted to talk to him about.

Just about anyone can be a trainer. The first thing you have to do is find someone with more money than sense, and take him to the sales.

'That's a nice sort,' you tell him. 'Trot him up and down a bit, would you? He's a bit shouldery, I don't think we'd better go above 70,000 guineas.' If the horse turns out to be no good, you can always sell him a year later for 2,000 guineas, which is what all the best bloodstock agents do. It doesn't seem to embarrass them.

At the stables, you get up early, march over to the yard, are beastly to the lads, drive up to the gallops in a Range Rover, get out, put on an enigmatic smile, stare through your binoculars and think, 'I wonder which one that is?' Then you tell some of the riders to go half-speed and others to go full-speed and, after you've bollocked them for going the wrong speed, you go home and have an enormous cooked breakfast. When you've finished that, you answer calls from your owners.

'It was my fault, Mr Weinstock. I thought I saw one of his legs fall off on the way to the start, but you know what it is with all those legs, you can never be quite sure. Anyway, I couldn't be more pleased with him now; the vet put him down last night.'

After that, you enter a couple of horses for races, read the *Sporting Life*, think about making an illegal proposal to the nanny and then pop out for a spot of lunch and a snorter in preparation for your afternoon nap. If any owners turn up for evening stables, you walk round with them, feel the horses' legs and tell the lad, 'There's a bit of heat in his fetlock. Poultice it up and stay up with him for the next three nights, would you?' Then you take the owners back to the house for a livener.

'Have another glass of champagne, Mr Abdullah. You really are a wonderful fellow, and such lovely colours. Do you still own Saudi Arabia?'

'No, Mr Sangster, I wouldn't put more than a couple of grand on it. I've told the jockey to wait until Catterick next month.'

On the whole, owners are to be discouraged from doing anything more strenuous than signing cheques, unless, of course, you are one, in which case the correct procedure is to phone your trainer every day and visit every week. Since it can't be your horse that is fit only for the inside of a cat, it must be the trainer. It's best to let him know that he's being watched.

When you arrive on the gallops, you'll see a lot of other owners all desperately trying to work out which one is theirs.

'Which one's mine, Mr Gosden?'

'They're all yours, Mr Mohammed.'

'It's that big brown one, in front, isn't it? He's looking good, isn't he?'

'Yes, isn't he just? Yours is the one at the back. I think he's just gone lame.'

It's a terrible disappointment when you visit your horse in his box and he doesn't recognise you. So you stand there thinking, 'I wonder what would happen if he kicked me,' and 'The stable lass has got a nice bum.' Then you realise the trainer has just said something and is waiting for you to say something back. It's better to play safe with, 'He's looking well, isn't he?', rather than kick off with, 'Isn't he a nice colour?' or 'Has he had his breakfast yet?'

Wait until your second visit before you wade in with, 'The way I see it, we'll run him down the pan a few times and then have a tremendous wallop in a Catterick seller. What do you think?'

It's vital that you don't confuse what the trainer says with what he really thinks. It's all in the nuances.

'I don't think he's an early type,' roughly translates as: Give me a ring in six months time and I'll tell you whether I'm going to run him this season or not.

'He's done nothing wrong.' He hasn't been arrested yet.

'He's wintered well.' It's almost April and he's still alive.

'He's a bit of a lad.' So far, he's killed two stable lads and demolished a set of starting stalls. We still can't get him to go in them, though.

'He's a good doer.' He can't run to save his life but, God, you should see him eat.

'I think he'll win a small race.' You'd be amazed how awful some of those sellers are at Folkestone.

For me, racing has always been about the racecourse and the betting shop, and it seemed strange when I read that Noel Murless, one of the great post-war trainers, preferred to stay at home. There wasn't even a Ladbrokes where he lived. It wasn't until I spoke to Brian Procter, and visited Bill Wightman's Hampshire yard, that it began to dawn on me that half the heart of racing lay hidden away from public view, miles from the racetracks, in tucked away stableyards and out-of-sight gallops.

B. Procter was one of the unnoticed names racing is full of. His name appeared in the racecards in the *Sporting Life*, next to the names of horses trained by Dick Hern; the ones that weren't going to win. Procter wanted to ride winners – that was what he had come into racing for – but he hadn't made it. Every season, he rode one, or two, occasionally four or five winners, never more. The only one I can remember was at Newbury in 1978. Dick Hern had two runners in the same race, which was why Procter had a ride. Willie Carson rode Lord Porchester's Bluebell, the 7–4 favourite, and Procter rode the Queen's debutante, Light O'Battle, Highclere's sister, but utterly unfancied at 33–1. At home, Light O'Battle was temperamental and regularly tailed off, and Hern's orders were to try not to finish last, for Her Majesty's sake.

As they turned into the straight, Light O'Battle started to labour, so Procter hit her a couple of times and began to push. He thought she might beat one. Halfway up the straight, he thought she might finish fourth. A bit further on, he had high hopes of third. Then he spotted Carson, in front of him on Bluebell. Carson's stick was up and he was getting ready to apply the kitchen sink, before really getting down to business. Watching from the stands, Willie looked like a whirling dervish, while Procter's mount was firmly on the bridle, for all the world as if her rider was shouting across, 'Go on, Willie. For God's sake, go on.' In fact, Procter was just making sure that Light O'Battle wasn't given the opportunity to turn down the giddy chance of victory; he put her nose in front right on the line. When they walked back to the unsaddling enclosure, Procter looked as if it was his worst day of the month, and even a large magnifying glass wouldn't have shown you much sign of celebration in the winner's enclosure.

Procter wasn't there to ride winners, he was there to ride difficult horses and educate ignorant ones. Hern didn't employ him for what he could do on the racecourse, he employed him for what he could do at home, on the gallops at West Ilsley. On the gallops, where, for every horse, there comes a day when the trainer finds out how good or, more often, how bad the beast is. Good trainers don't race their horses on the gallops, they make them fit, educate them, test them, an unknown quantity against a known quantity, bad against bad, good against good, gradually finding out a little more, without spoiling them. And not just how good they are, but how the horse moves, how it settles, if it does, whether it might be better ridden from behind or in front, what ground it likes, or dislikes.

Work riders have to know what pace to go; what the trainer means when he says, 'steady half speed,' or 'a good piece of work'. If you set off too fast at the bottom of an uphill gallop and make young horses tired and disappointed before they reach the top, you may spoil them. Riders have to work up gradually. Good horses reveal themselves without the need to gallop flat out. It's a feel, an easiness in their work. A good horse picks up, is smooth and within himself, lengthens and stretches and needs only a gentle asking. Procter rode some very good horses at home, on the gallops: Bustino and Highclere, Dunfermline, Troy and Henbit, Ela-Mana-Mou and Bireme, Sun Princess and Unfuwain, Brigadier Gerard and Nashwan. On the gallops, Brigadier Gerard would doddle along, doddle along and then Procter would pull him out from behind the lead horse, and the Brigadier would fly past, easy, relaxed.

One April day in 1989, Procter and Carson set off together to the start of the trial ground, a one-mile gallop running alongside the Ridgeway. Procter was riding Misbah, a highly rated four-year-old; Carson was riding a three-year-old called Nashwan. Procter followed Hern's instructions, which were to build up to a good, strong piece of work. With two furlongs to go, Nashwan passed Misbah and strode into a distant speck.

In all his many years at West Ilsley, Procter had never seen anything like it. Usually, when a rider asks a horse to quicken, the jockey's backside drops into the saddle and he urges and kicks his mount forward. When Nashwan flew past, Carson was standing up in the irons, as if he was cantering to the start. Nashwan was soon gone, and so were the fancy prices for the Two Thousand Guineas. Procter wasn't someone who tumbled words out for the pleasure of it. He held on to them until he was sure they said what he wanted them to. 'Nashwan is definitely the best horse I have ever sat on,' he told me.

Better than any horse Bill Wightman trained, up on Stephens Castle Downs, in Hampshire. For Wightman, training was a way of life embedded in the countryside. We stood on his beautiful downland turf and watched and listened in the quiet of the breeze. The landscape stretched away in sweeping hollows, without a building in sight, just swooping swifts and yellow cowslips. Wightman let his four black dogs jump out of the back of his tatty estate car and picked up a garden fork. There had been no rain for four weeks but, as the string of five horses cantered by, Wightman pushed the fork easily into the old grassland.

Nothing had changed there for fifty years and Wightman, quiet, accepting, blended perfectly into the setting he had become a part of, utterly at home, with his horses and the swifts, in the sun and the breeze. Wightman was patient, and relished the rewards of patience. He liked to set his battered cap at one of the big handicaps and work his way towards it. He liked to watch a horse improving, so tangibly that you could almost see it, day by day. And he was good at it. The Portland Handicap with Privateer and Walk By, the Ayr Gold Cup with Somersway, the Cambridgeshire with Flying Nelly, the Wokingham and Stewards' Cup with Import, the Newbury Spring Cup and John Smith's Magnet Cup with Air Trooper, and, finally, after fielding three successive runners-up, the Lincoln with King's Ride.

When his horses were past racing, he put them in a paddock near his picturesque farmhouse, and visited them every day. Wightman called them his pensioners, and Wightman's pensioners never left Ower Farm. It was one of the rules. They lived out their lives where their trainer could see that they were well looked after and, if they had to be put down, they were put down at home and buried beneath the lawn in front of the house.

Bill Wightman liked to see the result of his labours on the racecourse but, if you wanted to understand a trainer like him, you had to go to Stephens Castle Downs. That is one of the things I have learned about racing. To understand it, you have to leave the racecourse, and travel to stableyards and gallops.

# Chapter Nine

## Tigers

While work proceeded on my best-seller, 'Records of Achievement in the Marketplace', I made three trips into London, to an office, a hotel, and an apartment, and a fourth one to the country. They were all visits to satisfy curiosity.

The office, in Sloane Street, was ringed by tigers, elephants, and Sumatran rhinoceroses, thankfully in statue form; but there was something alive and black under the desk, possibly a jaguar. I wouldn't have been surprised, since John Aspinall once kept a tigress called Tara in his flat in Eaton Place, along with a capuchin monkey and two Himalayan bears. He exercised them in Eaton Square.

Aspinall is best known for his conviction that, as long as you treat them right, tigers make good room-mates. Every now and again one of the tigers at Aspinall's zoo kills one of its keepers, causing the zoo's owner to scratch his head before reasserting his conviction that, as long as you treat them right, tigers make good room-mates.

Physically imposing and charismatic, an interesting rather than a nice man, amusing and amused, Aspinall had just relaunched himself as a bookmaker, with a logo embracing his two passions. The logo showed a gorilla holding a plate bearing the inscription 'In Ludo Veritas': in gaming lies truth. It was not Aspinall's first venture into bookmaking. That came forty years earlier, after he had pursued an Oxford tripos made up of poker, horses and greyhounds. Mornings were devoted to the study of poker, afternoons to the horses, evenings to the dogs, then back round to poker again. Aspinall missed his final examinations, because they coincided with Royal Ascot, but he did learn one valuable lesson, the one that has passed many of us by: punters lose money, bookmakers make it.

Aspinall joined up with Ian Maxwell-Scott, famous for being a descendant of Sir Walter Scott, and made his way to the back row of the Silver Ring at Plumpton. The new firm attracted business by offering 13–8 when everyone else was going 6–4, and soon found out why no one else was doing the same. Maxwell-Scott retired hurt, but Aspinall ploughed on, issuing tickets proclaiming 'Aspers Never Owes'. In 1953, when he was twenty-seven, Aspinall made £10,000, a sum so large for its vintage that it was almost enough to sustain him in Room 505 of the Ritz. Almost.

A great raconteur, Aspinall found his niche in staging high-class gambling parties for the sons of aristocrats ready and willing to be parted from their parents' money. Appearance was all. While Aspinall arranged for the wall of a Mayfair flat to be covered with Canalettos and Panninis, on approval from a local art gallery, his mother, Lady Osborne, supplied game pie. In eighteen months, Aspinall's much sought-after chemmy games made him £350,000, supplemented by a thumping win on Prelone, at 20–1, in the 1956 Cesarewitch. It was a lot of money to get rid of, unless you had set your heart on restoring Howletts estate in Kent and filling it with wild animals, the sort that liked to eat the odd keeper.

Eventually, the police raided one of Aspinall's chemmy

games, accusing him of keeping a common gaming house. Lady Osborne informed the policeman, 'Young man, there was nothing common here until you walked in.' The case was dismissed.

It was unfortunate that Aspinall lost all his money on Wall Street just before he opened the Clermont Club, but with Annabel's downstairs and Lord Lucan looking like a Lord upstairs (until the trouble with the nanny), he soon got it back again. Then the 1968 Gaming Act, with its tighter controls, destroyed much of the pleasure Aspinall derived from running a casino; so, in 1972, he sold the Clermont Club and invested most of the proceeds in the 1973 financial crash.

In 1978, he opened Little Aspinall's, not for the fun of it, but for the finances of it. By 1981, it was making £8 million a year, and Aspinall expanded into the Curzon House Club. Six years later, he sold the Club for £90 million, enough to feed his wild animals for several years.

Aspinall was sixty-three when he reverted to bookmaking. He didn't need the money, but he needed the stimulation, and gambling and the company of gamblers supplied it.

'If a man is a gambler,' Aspinall opined, 'it's an enormous start with me.' Me too. We didn't have much else in common, but some of the things Aspinall had to say about gambling echoed my own thoughts.

'One of the qualities I like,' Aspinall told me, 'is that gamblers don't respect money like other people do. They appreciate the necessity of having money, but they don't revere it.' In Aspinall's mind, gamblers were lined up in battle formation against 'all those boring, middle-class, Calvinistic, Puritanic ideas about the sanctity of money. Among gamblers, you can borrow or lend easily, without loss of pride. There's a free-masonry among gamblers, a cameraderie that is wonderful.' The sinner isn't the gambler, careless with his money, but the man with the carefully monitored purse and book-keeping mind.

Aspinall was said to have spent £400,000 on his sixtieth birthday party, in 1986, but was unrepentant, drawing on Keynesian economics to justify the extravagance.

'Think where the money went. To car hire firms, florists, fruiterers, agencies for hiring dwarfs. It wasn't burnt or put in an account. None of it was wasted.

'People said, "What unbelievable extravagance." Thank God people are extravagant. The rich man should spend. He should leave a wake of expenditure in his path. It's terrible when rich men don't, but become seized up on making more and more money, and doing nothing with it. That's very dull. I avoid people like that, particularly if they don't gamble.'

Paul Mellon didn't need to gamble, and wasn't a gambler by nature, but he didn't let his money, and there was plenty of it, sit idly in a vault. He spent some of it on a string of 100 racehorses and, characteristically, felt uneasy about it, a feeling Aspinall would never have experienced. 'I love my horses and love to see them run,' Mellon wrote in his autobiography, 'but I sometimes still feel guilty about it because it is a luxury and an economically useless hobby.'

I knew Mellon, indirectly, twenty years before meeting him: through his colours. His colours were the reason I wanted to meet him. You couldn't miss them; black with a gold cross and stripe on cap. They were everywhere, and they were carried to eternal glory by Mill Reef, along with a sheepskin noseband.

When I first met him, in a London hotel, Mellon was impeccably dressed and courteous, like other wealthy men mellowing into old age. What made him different was his shyness and humility. Mellon was a modest, self-aware man, who knew his own limitations. These are not easy qualities to hang on to when you are head of one of the three richest families in America, along with the Rockefeller and Ford dynasties. The same qualities shone through in Mellon's ghosted autobiography, *Reflections in a Silver Spoon*. It was a brave and honest book, about a man born with a silver ladle in his mouth, who knew that he was not a clever man and never conquered doubts about his own worth.

It was while Mellon was at Cambridge University that he developed his love of hunting and racing and sporting art. The first painting he bought was 'Pumpkin', by George Stubbs. It remained his favourite picture, but is now worth a lot more than the $5,000 he paid for it in the 1930s.

In 1936 Mellon sent Drinmore Lad, a successful chaser in America, to Ivor Anthony's stable at Kingsclere, near Newbury. Sixty years later, Mellon still had horses in training at the same yard, where Ivor Anthony had been succeeded first by Peter Hastings-Bass and then by Ian Balding.

Not all wealthy owners are loved by their trainers, but Mellon was so popular at the yard that John Matthias, the stable jockey in the late 1970s and early 1980s, didn't have a bad word to say about him even after Mellon had sacked him. He described Mellon to me as 'a lovely man, a marvellous man'. In 1981, several jockeys were trying to edge their seats into Glint Of Gold's saddle for the Derby, but Mellon stuck by Matthias, who rode Glint Of Gold into a creditable second place behind Shergar. The next season, when Matthias lost three big races he acknowledged he should have won, Mellon took the trouble to explain to him why he would not be riding his best horses the following year. That counted with Matthias, who carried on riding the owner's lesser lights. It said it all that, in 1972, when Balding phoned Mellon to tell him that his lifetime champion, Mill Reef, had broken a leg on the gallops, Mellon's first reaction was to ask if the lad was all right.

Like Mellon, Sir Hugh Dundas was modest and unassuming, with the self-deprecating humour that seems to accompany courage. When I walked into his Knightsbridge flat, I had no idea that this diffident-seeming six-foot-four-inch beanpole concealed a man brave beyond belief.

I arrived simply curious to know who it was who half-owned Ghofar, the winner of the 1989 Hennessy Gold Cup. He turned out not only to be Lord Oaksey's brother-in-law and the former chairman and chief executive of the BET conglomerate, but also far more than that.

If Lady Dundas hadn't prompted and prodded him, her husband would never have mentioned it, but when I left, he gave me a signed copy of a book published the previous year, called *Flying Start*. It was the account of a young fighter pilot's struggle to reconcile his 'sincere desire to engage the enemy' with his equally 'sincere desire to stay alive', in circumstances which made it extremely difficult to do both. Hugh Dundas was nineteen years old when Messerschmitts first fired on the Spitfire he was piloting over Dunkirk; nineteen. When he was twenty, he was shot down, twice, experiencing the panic and terror, fear and confusion of spinning earthwards fast in a smoke-filled cockpit.

'Death stretched out its hand to touch me every day,' he wrote. 'Everybody was frightened, and everybody knew that everybody else was frightened.'

He lent me some photographs. One showed a group containing Douglas Bader, another showed Hugh and his brother John sitting on the garden steps of their parents' home in Yorkshire in the autumn of 1940, a few weeks before his brother was killed.

During a two-month spell in the summer of 1941, Dundas's squadron lost over half its pilots. By then, Dundas had been awarded the DFC and promoted to Flight Lieutenant, soon to become Flight Commander, Squadron Commander and, at the age of twenty-two, Wing Commander.

When Dundas had finished teetering on the cotton thin line which divided life from death, he was sent to Malta, Sicily and, finally, Italy, to repeat the same macabre balancing act. In 1944, aged twenty-four, Dundas became the youngest ever Group Captain. In the same year, he was awarded the DSO and, in 1945, a bar to go with it.

Dundas felt fear, but faced it down. He led from the front, trying to hold his men's terror in check. In Italy, using their Spitfires as fighter bombers, the pilots had to resist the compelling urge to veer away from the endless succession of ground targets and the heavy flak every attack provoked. No skill could be employed to evade it. Pilots simply clung to the hope that they would be lucky. With good luck, you would be hit but manage to get home, as Dundas did twice. With bad luck, you would be forced to bale out or crash land. With no luck, you would be killed.

It was a setting ripe for grim comedy. Bombs arrived with faulty fuses, blowing up the planes that were carrying them. Dundas himself was almost shot down by a British pilot who, nerves in shreds, opened fire on his own commander.

He died in 1995, after another brave battle, this time against cancer. Brave owners, brave jockeys, brave both.

Edward Cazalet sent me directions. Turn left for Wivelsfield Green and Plumpton. Then on to Plumpton Green, the Plough, and Shaw Farm, Cazalet's country residence.

Cazalet had once been a competent amateur rider, winning the 1958 Kim Muir Chase at Cheltenham on Lochroe, trained by his father Peter, and he had recently been appointed a High Court judge, but the purpose of my visit was to talk not about his own achievements, but those of his late godfather, Anthony Mildmay, a near-mythical figure in racing. Cazalet showed me albums and scrapbooks devoted to the halcyon days of Fairlawne, the mansion in Kent where Peter Cazalet trained, and Lord Mildmay learned to ride.

Like Paul Mellon, Mildmay was born with a silver service in

his mouth; like Hugh Dundas, he was tall and thin, the wrong shape entirely for a jockey.

The second Baron Mildmay of Flete enjoyed a childhood inhabited by a nanny, a nurserymaid, a butler, a coachman, second horseman and a succession of French governesses. He met Peter Cazalet at Eton, but they had little in common. Cazalet was a gifted athlete who won blues at Oxford in cricket, tennis, squash and rackets, and later turned down the offer of the captaincy of Kent County Cricket Club. Mildmay was also a keen sportsman but neither looked, nor was, the part: a tall, thin, gangling figure, his ungraceful movements were the legacy of a childhood attack of rickets. He managed to win a point-to-point race while at Cambridge in the late 1920s, but was no great horseman.

After university, Mildmay arranged to ride out at Fairlawne before travelling into the City each day. In 1933, in the same month that he rode his first winner under Rules, Mildmay made his debut in the Grand National, on board Cazalet's Youtell. While Cazalet completed the awesome course on Shaun Goilin, the 1930 winner, Mildmay fell at the first fence and broke his nose. He then decided that it was time to give up – not racing, but the City; for what Mildmay lacked in natural ability, which was a lot, he made up for in enthusiasm, nerve and determination. From then on, Mildmay lived for long periods at Fairlawne, working to improve his riding and becoming a much-loved member of Cazalet's family.

For both men, winning the Grand National became a major ambition. In 1936, Mildmay nearly succeeded on Davy Jones. The horse went off at 100–1 but, two fences from home, he had the measure of Reynoldstown, the previous year's winner, when he pecked on landing and Mildmay slipped the reins. Normally, he rode with a knot in them. That day, he didn't. The buckle failed, the reins flapped loose, and Davy Jones ran out at the final fence.

Defeat was the making of Mildmay as a public figure. Whatever he felt, he didn't complain. Instead, he thanked the fates, who didn't deserve it, for giving him a memorable ride. The British loved him for losing so gallantly.

During the war, Mildmay and Cazalet both served with distinction in the Welsh Guards. On their return, they threw themselves into the task of turning Fairlawne into a major National Hunt stable. Cazalet was the driving force, with a well-earned reputation for thoroughness and a taste for the virtues of a distinctly military stable regime. Punctuality and highly polished boots were in; long hair and sharing a breakfast table with jockeys were out. Old-fashioned master–servant relationships lived on at Fairlawne, and many of the staff were content with the ancien régime. Jim Fairgrieve, Cazalet's head lad, Bill Braddon, the travelling head lad, and lads such as John Hole, who joined the yard before the Second World War, were still there thirty years later.

Mildmay worked away at his unpromising physique and became a stronger, more secure rider. The racing public loved his courage, modesty, and will to win. 'Come on, m'Lord!' And he did come on, until he was good enough to win the amateur riders' championship five times, and be a match for the professionals.

In 1947, at Folkestone, a fall from the ominously named Fatal Rock caused permanent damage to Mildmay's neck and left him vulnerable to sudden, crippling attacks of cramp. At the Canal Turn in the 1948 Grand National, an attack forced Mildmay's chin to his chest and rendered him a helpless passenger. Cromwell, Mildmay's favourite horse, carried him into third place. In 1949, again on Cromwell, he finished fourth; the following year, the pair fell. Shortly afterwards, aged forty-one, Anthony Mildmay was overcome by cramp when swimming in Devon, and drowned.

In a much-quoted tribute from his closest friend, Cazalet

described Mildmay as a man who 'refused to be daunted by misfortune or spoilt by success'. To Edward Cazalet, who, as a boy, had worshipped him, Mildmay was 'a golden character, enormously kind and very unassuming, as far from being arrogant as could be. He and my father raced for fun.' Their spirit of enjoyment was instrumental in attracting the Queen Mother to jump racing at a time when it was very much the poor relation of the Flat. Together, the three of them gave a tremendous boost to the sport.

After Mildmay's death, his friends presented a Challenge Trophy for the Mildmay Memorial Handicap Chase, to be run as a trial for the Grand National, at Sandown Park each January. The first race was run in 1952 and Cromwell, by then an eleven-year-old, lined up with Bryan Marshall wearing Mildmay's light blue and white hoops. For once, the fates knew what was required of them. It was one of the most emotional of occasions. As Edward Cazalet remembered, 'The image of Anthony Mildmay riding past the winning post was so clear in the memory of those there, that to see his colours going past the winning post seemed like a tribute.'

Peter Cazalet trained for another twenty years, winning more than 250 races for the Queen Mother, but he was best known for yet another Grand National defeat, when Devon Loch snatched defeat from the jaws of victory in 1956, to bring back memories of Davy Jones, Cromwell and Lord Mildmay. Where Fairlawne and the National were concerned, there was to be no happy ending.

Like Mildmay, Cazalet combined good fortune at birth with his fair share of misfortune thereafter. His first wife and elder brother both died during the Second World War, and in his sixties, Cazalet himself was struck down by cancer. After his death in 1973 the Queen Mother transferred her horses to Fulke Walwyn, but she never raced on the same scale again. It was fitting that the name of the race held in Mildmay's honour was changed to the Anthony Mildmay–Peter Cazalet Memorial Steeplechase, and it was the name of the race that first aroused my curiosity.

The race is still run at Sandown Park every January, and the dwindling band who can remember life at Fairlawne meet each year to celebrate the memory.

## Chapter Ten

# Dear Mort . . . Situation is . . .

'Records of Achievement in the Marketplace' safely on the best-seller list, I moved on to 'Strategic Quality Management in Essex Colleges and the Local Education Authority'. This made me one of only five people in Britain who knew what strategic quality management was. Now, it's down to four.

That August, 1990, I went to the Eighth International Conference on Risk and Gambling, where I discovered that Johnnie Johnson and Alistair Bruce had been investigating 'Successful Betting Strategies'. Johnson and Bruce had examined a huge pile of betting slips and concluded that the only way to make money was to wait until thirty seconds before the off, and then take the board price. They seemed to think that punters who hung on until the last half-minute were operating on an elevated analytical plane. We all know that, when the last show is 7–2, the starting price is 3–1 if the horse wins and 4–1 if it loses, but I still wasn't altogether convinced.

What punters were actually doing was dashing round the betting shop trying to find a biro that worked, trying to find the right page in the *Sporting Life* so that they could stick the biro into the list of runners, trying to find the counter, and then trying, desperately, to persuade the cashier to take the bet even though half the field had already covered three furlongs and the race was only five furlongs long.

So I drifted off to another promising presentation, on the new American craze of video poker. The American researcher's face was named after the game, and he explained, apologetically, that, for methodological reasons, it had been necessary to play the machines himself. He needed to watch the players playing and the best way of doing this, without looking out of place, was to join in. So he approached a machine, put a reluctant dollar in the slot, and pressed a button. Five cards appeared on the screen. Three of them were the Ace of Spades, King of Spades and Jack of Spades. It paid $15,000; straight up.

'What can you do with that sort of money?' po-face asked his audience. I didn't say anything, but I'd have thought it was pretty obvious. You give half to your bookmaker, to stop him wondering whether it isn't time to call in the heavies, and whack the rest on a stone-bonking certainty in the seller at Pontefract.

'I set it off against the mortgage,' he said. That must have been exciting.

Between papers on 'Predicting Casino Revenue Using Stochastic Migration Simulation' and 'Psychothanitoid Syndrome: Why Treatment Sometimes Fails' was a presentation by John Mort Green, 'The Aussie Bookie: The Art and Social Distinction of Bookmaking On Course, Down Under.' A tall, slim, grey-haired Australian stood up with a bookmaker's board and talked about betting in Queensland. He delivered an opening I came to know, and love. 'Situation is . . .'

John Mort Green, alias The Butterfly, known as Papillon in France and Cho Chosan in Japan, loved life, and had lived it. A showman, a storyteller, a maker of phrases, a life-enhancer, a one-off.

'Situation is,' said Mort, sitting at the bar of the Royal Garden Hotel in Kensington in his pink shirt, floral necktie and red cardigan. 'I've never done a day's work in my life.' This was because, long ago, in Queensland, Mort discovered something about bookmakers and jockeys. There was one bookmaker in particular, a cautious man, not given to laying over the odds. But Mort noticed that, now and again, he did lay over the odds, and always on the same jockey's mounts. The mounts always lost, and the bookmaker always won, and Mort won with him.

In 1963, Mort gathered up his swag, flew to London and booked in at the White House in Regent's Park.

In those days, some of Europe's top riders came from Australia: Bill Williamson and Bill Pyers, Russ Maddock and George Moore, Scobie Breasley, Ron Hutchinson, Garnie Bougoure and Pat Glennon. They were a long way from home, not all the jockeys in the weighing room were nice to them, and they welcomed the sight of a friendly Australian face. 'Horses don't talk but jockeys do,' says Mort. 'They were my bread and butter.' Those were good days, days when Mort's hands moved between the steering wheel of a Rolls-Royce, the neck of a champagne bottle and the waist of a pretty girl.

One day in 1964, Mort got a phone call from Paris. It was Pat Glennon, who rode for Etienne Pollet. 'There's a horse I want you to come over and look at,' said Glennon. 'He won't be beaten next year, but he's too fractious to send to England, he'll win the French Derby.' The horse was called Sea Bird II.

The English and French Derbys were run within eight days of each other. Convinced that Sea Bird II, who had won the Prix Lupin in devastating style, would go to Chantilly for the French Derby, English bookmakers pushed out his Epsom price to 20–1, a carrot for mug-money.

Less than two weeks before the Derby, Mort received another

phone call. It was Glennon. 'That you, Butterfly? I galloped him today and they've changed their minds. We're coming to England and I'll be riding; green jacket, black cap.'

Mort borrowed a set of overalls from the janitor at the White House, dirtied his hands, pulled a hat down over his eyes, and set off round London on a bus, stopping off at every betting shop he could find. He didn't open his mouth, and he didn't put more than £8 on in one go. By the time he handed back the overalls, he had got £860 on, all at 20–1. You could buy a house for £860. Mort was in the market for a whole street.

In those days, racing papers paid scant attention to what was happening in France. Peter O'Sullevan was the first journalist to break the news of Sea Bird II's cross-channel trip, and the French challenger's price promptly tumbled to 8–1, then 5–1, 3–1 hard to get.

Sea Bird II was highly strung and Glennon had warned, 'The only thing that can beat this horse is the parade. If I can get him down to the start OK, he won't be beaten.' He went down like a lamb and came back like a champion. Watching from the stand as the Derby field rounded Tattenham Corner, Mort turned to his companion and said, 'Time and margin.'

'What do you mean?'

'He's won. The only question is, how far?'

Sea Bird II beat the best England had to offer without bothering to come off the bridle. When he had brushed aside the strongest field ever assembled for the Prix de l'Arc de Triomphe, Glennon walked into the weighing room at Longchamp, threw his saddle on the floor and told his audience, 'I've ridden at Alice Springs, and I've ridden at Darwin, but wherever I ride I will never ride a better horse than this. I am going to retire; that was my last ride.'

While Glennon went home to Australia, bought a fishing boat and sailed over the horizon, The Butterfly got a taxi to the Bank of America, unlocked the safe deposit box where he had lodged his winnings, and took out £22,000. Multiply by ten for today's equivalent. Then he went to Thomas Cook and booked a world tour. 'Grand de luxe,' Mort insisted. The tour started on the *Queen Mary*, took in New York, Florida, California, Hawaii, Japan, Hong Kong and Bombay, and wound up, six months later, in Beirut.

Mort was sixty-one when I met him; there was a twinkle in his eye and a jauntiness in his step and energy to spare. The next time I met him was at Royal Ascot. Mort had just arrived from Switzerland, where he had met an Arab Sheikh, and bet with him on the French Open tennis.

'Shot by shot,' said Mort, in his Brisbane twang. '6–4 the server, 6–4 the receiver, 6–1 an ace on the first serve, 33–1 an ace on the second. I'm full of money.';

Mort was standing in box 185, dressed in a chef's uniform, with a green bow tie and a big white hat. 'Tough times never last,' said Mort, 'but tough people do.' I preferred another epigram he had pinned on the wall: 'One thing you learn about being broke is that you don't want to be broke for long.'

The Sheikh had lent Mort an apartment in Belgravia, and when I visited him there he was wearing his archdeacon's outfit, with a purple shirt and gold cross. 'I pray every night,' Mort explained, 'and all my prayers start with, "Please God, save me from tomorrow's good thing." ' Mort claimed to have read the Bible eleven times. I don't know whether he had or not, but every one of his letters was adorned with a sticker bearing a quotation from the Bible, or from his own Bible. Once, when I tipped him a winner at Newbury, he forced an envelope into my shirt pocket. 'Little gratuity for you,' said Mort. On the envelope was a quotation. 'When He has tried me I shall come forth as gold. Job 23:10.' Then he showed me a photograph starring Mort, in his archdeacon's gear, standing in front of a green double-decker bus. Most of the top of the bus was taken up with a sign reading 'Jesus The Lord'.

'I was six months with God's Green Bus in California, giving them this,' Mort explained, pursing his lips and moving them up and down very quickly. 'You've got to say the words right. They loved the way I said "Calvary" – Kal-Varrey. I had their eyes rolling in their sockets.' Mort paused, a rare pause. 'Myself, I don't believe in God.'

Without another pause, Mort turned round and said, 'This is South London Linda.' Linda was slim, blonde, from South London, and in a bathrobe. She had just got out of a jacuzzi as big as the Ritz, in a bathroom with glass wallpaper, where I later watched myself being bald from ten different angles. Linda smiled and Mort carried on. 'Situation is, Linda plays backgammon. She goes into a London club; a posh club, you understand. All men. Beautiful woman.' Mort turned and looked approvingly at South London Linda, who smiled approvingly back. ' "I'll play you," says Linda. Big smile, flutters the eyelashes. Big, long eyelashes, you understand. "As long as it's not for too much." The men think it's going to be a game of tennis. Lots of bravado. Linda's fluttering her eyelashes. Then she turns the men upside down and empties their trouser pockets. She's a good player.' Mort turned to Linda. Linda nodded. Then I nodded, to show that I understood.

Mort switched the video on. 'Eagle Farm, June eighth,' he said. The race started. Mort kept tapping the screen with a knife. 'Champagne King, you got him?' I'd got him. 'Waiting for this for two months,' said Mort. 'Four thousand down. Bit of 9–2, rest at 4–1.' I worked it out, roughly. Yes, it was quite a lot.

Mick Dittman, Australia's champion jockey was on board, thrash, thrash, thrashing away with his whip. Five yards out, the horse on the rail looked certain to win. Three yards out, it was looking like the fast finisher on the outside. Two inches out, Champagne King took it up and won by a short half-head.

'Pulling clear, wasn't he?' said Mort. 'I was coming to Ascot anyway, but that was the icing on the cake; the icing on the cake.'

'And a cherry, Mort. One of those big red cherries, on the top.'

'I don't want you to think they're all winning stories,' said Mort. 'I've got a losing story for you, later.'

As well as the jacuzzi, and wardrobes full of the Sheikh's silk shirts, the apartment came with a very big car and a fairly big driver, called Michel or Michelle as Mort liked to call him. Michelle was a swarthy Algerian, who looked as if he had worked for a drug company in Marseilles. 'Big heart,' said Mort, 'like Linda.' Unless you play backgammon, I thought.

Mort, South London Linda and I got into the Rolls-Royce, 7 HRH, and Michelle drove us to Maxwell's Fish and Chip Restaurant opposite Belsize Park station, where we sat on the pavement eating fish and chips and drinking Chablis.

'Halibut, no chips,' Mort had told Maxwell, before telling us about Baldric II and Ginger Meggs.

Ginger Meggs was Bill Pyers' nickname. Ginger because he had ginger hair, and Meggs because Meggs was a famous comic strip character in Australia, with buck teeth, like Pyers. Baldric II was trained by Ernie Fellows, in France, and Pyers had won both the Two Thousand Guineas and Champion Stakes on him in 1964.

'Nineteen sixty-five,' said Mort, 'early on. Situation is, Ginger Meggs tells me that Baldric II's going to win a lovely race for us, and then be off to stud. The race was to be the Jockey Club Stakes, at Newmarket, in April.

'But it was a bad winter in England, and the horses weren't ready. There'd be no competition. "No coup," I said to Bill, "put the shutters down." But Baldric II was owned by Mrs Howell Jackson, and she wanted him to run. So, over he came, in the plane, with Bal Masque, his trial horse.

'We got the money ready, ready to go and, the night before

the race, Baldric II had colic, couldn't run. "Scratch them both, take them back to France," said Mrs Howell Jackson.

'Fellows tells her there are only three runners left, and Bal Masque might as well run for the third prize money. "Mr Fellows," said Mrs Howell Jackson, "these are the oldest racing colours in the State of Maryland. I am not having my colours disgraced at Newmarket." '

Mort broke off to tip the waitress. Mort was a great tipper. He liked to tip when the meal arrived, when the drinks arrived, when the plates were taken away, and when the pudding turned up.

'Eventually, she relented,' he carried on. 'The English didn't know what was happening. There was no French form in the papers. The smarties gave a wink and told each other, "Baldric's come over as a blind. Bal Masque's the horse."

'But I knew he wasn't. Hadn't run for eighteen months and he was a sprinter. His job was to lead Baldric II up the gallops for six furlongs. The Jockey Club Stakes was one and a half miles.

'Only three runners, and Bal Masque couldn't win. Could not win. Neither could Autre Prince. He was just a hurdler with Eric Cousins. Only one left. Tom Jones's horse, Le Pirate, with Bill Williamson up. He had a bit of form; he was a certainty.' The Butterfly leant across the pavement. 'An unbeatable certainty.'

'We're all armed to bet, and the bookies open up. It's evens Bal Masque, and 6–4 Le Pirate. 6–4 Le Pirate! In we go. Le Pirate in to evens, Bal Masque out to 5–1. Money everywhere.

'They come on down into the dip and Bal Masque is still in front – a sprinter, hasn't run for eighteen months. Billy Pyers up. They hit the rising ground, and he's still in front. Williamson starts to get busy on Le Pirate, but it's no good.

'As they're pulling up, Bill looks across at Ginger Meggs and says, "If we'd gone round again, you'd still have won." '

Mort leaned back, to give us time to let it sink in, and then rounded it off.

'All the smarties think we backed Bal Masque off course; backed Le Pirate on course to fix the odds, but we didn't, we were penniless; penniless. In the car back, Billy Pyers said to me, "What could I do?" "I love this sport," I told him, "but you've got to find money for it, and you've got to wipe your hand across your mouth." '

Mort turned to me, and smiled. 'Tenacity of purpose,' he said, 'and the will to win. That's what saw me through.'

Whenever I see him now, Mort gives me a card, with his latest homespun philosophy staring up through the plastic. 'Laugh often. It is life's lubricant.' 'Plan as though you will live for ever. You will.' Once, I mentioned Blossom Dearie to him and, a few days later, a tape arrived. On one side was a recording of Blossom playing at Ronnie Scott's. 'Now I'm deep into Zen meditation and macrobiotics and, as soon as I can, I intend to get into narcotics.' On the other side were recordings of Mort's favourite finishes to Australian Derbys.

A couple of weeks later, I found myself watching a video of Mort winning a camel race in Queensland.

Dear old Blossom; dear one and only Mort.

## Chapter Eleven

# Racing Via Vegas

Alastair Down asked if I would like to work for the *Sporting Life* full time, feature writing and news reporting, and arranged a meeting with Mike Gallemore, the editor. Forty-one, ready for a change, I said yes please and handed 'Reorganizing Post-16 Education: The Tertiary Option' to Barbara Tomlins. At the NFER they greeted the news with mild amusement. God knows what they made of it at the *Life*.

Luckily for me, I joined Nick Reeves, Gary Nutting and Mike Cattermole on the newsdesk, which meant that three out of the four of us knew what we were doing. One of the first calls I made was to Gordon Richards, who trained a promising chaser called Full Strength. 'How's Full Strength?' I asked him, which seemed a pretty safe question. 'Not reet well, lad. He broke his neck at Ascot three days ago.'

Shortly afterwards, a Newmarket trainer phoned up to let us know that Tom Waugh, a member of a famous family of trainers, had died. 'John Waugh will be able to tell you about him,' he said.

So I phoned John Waugh.

'I understand Tom Waugh's died,' I began.

'Died? Tom? Good lord, I only saw him the day before yesterday. He was hale and hearty then. James will be able to tell you more than I can. Good lord.'

So I phoned James Waugh. Mrs Waugh answered. 'Good God. Good God. You'd better speak to James.'

'I understand Tom's died,' I said.

'Dead! Dead! Good God. Tom? I only saw him yesterday afternoon. He seemed fine then. You'd better speak to Jack.'

So I phoned Jack Waugh, and told him the bad news. He burst out laughing. 'That's bloody amazing,' he said, 'because Tom walked out of my back door only five minutes ago.'

There was a great atmosphere on the newsdesk, buzzing with humour and enthusiasm, and I loved it. I even didn't mind Charles Wilson, the Mirror Group's managing director, who was nicknamed the Scotweiler. Charlie had a keen interest in horse racing and, in the early days, before Robert Maxwell fell through the bottom of his boat and forced Charlie to concentrate his considerable energies elsewhere, he took a personal interest in the *Sporting Life*. He'd ring up on Sunday mornings to check that you were chasing up what he thought you should be chasing up. The absence of a bollocking was highly prized. Wilson always looked as if he was about to sack you. One of the many stories circulating at the time focused on a particular timid sub-editor. Charlie took to asking him how he was.

'How are you, fingertips?'

'Very well, thank you, Mr Wilson.'

This went on, day after day, until, eventually, the sub-editor plucked up courage and said, 'Mr Wilson, why do you always call me fingertips?'

'Because that's what you're clinging on to your job by, laddie.'

Like many people, I'd never really known what I wanted to do; still didn't know at forty, beyond a nagging regret that I hadn't switched from history to law at university. When I was teaching, the first thing I said when I woke up every morning was 'Oh, dear.' All round the country, every morning, there are people waking up, saying 'Oh, dear.' Sometimes I question the value of writing about horse racing, but most of the time I don't. So many people long for Friday evening, dread Monday morning, hate the thought of going to work, wish it was time to go home, look at their watches. If you are not one of them, you are lucky.

Racing, as Phil Bull famously and rightly put it, is 'a great triviality', but that is as high as any sport rises, and in racing, you can do a Placepot. Now, for the first time, I was working with people who shared my interest in racing. It was OK to stand in the office and watch a race on television; it was OK to have a bet. You could watch the racing, and no one complained. They paid you for it.

It meant having to go to Royal Ascot, which I'd managed to avoid for twenty-five years, but it was a price worth paying. I'd avoided it because there were too few selling races and too many people I knew I'd want to assassinate, starting with the bowler-hatted gatemen, who kept sending me home for a jacket and tie. The British are obsessed with jackets and ties. They don't mind if you're a serial killer, as long as you've got a tie on. And when I was finally allowed inside, there was the appalling Mrs Shilling, her head covered in climbing spinach, waiting to appear on television.

I know I've mellowed in the last few years because I no longer feel an overwhelming urge to abuse all the people at Royal Ascot who stand gawping mindlessly at the space soon to be occupied by the royal procession. When it arrives, the carriages are full of people with ridiculous names, like the Earl de la Warr, and Dame Roma Mitchell. Most of them have double-barrelled surnames, which always makes me think, unfairly, that they must be stupid. How can anyone called Lieutenant Colonel

Seymour Gilbart-Denham expect to be taken seriously?

After you've joined the English aristocracy over a few bottles of champagne, you begin to see the point of it all, even though the price of the champagne rises as your ability to pay for it falls. The point is to gawp. The men stare at the women, and the women stare at the women, too, claws out. As I walked past two women, one said to the other, 'It does the same for her bosom. It pushes them so high, it's extraordinary.'

'There are some beautiful women here, aren't there?' I asked another journalist, pointlessly.

'Yes,' he said, gloomily, 'but it doesn't do you any good. It only makes you feel grumpy when you get home.'

Royal Ascot ends on a suitably Edwardian note, with people singing songs of Empire around the bandstand. It reminds me of Joan Littlewood's *Oh, What a Lovely War*. Then I want to start shooting people again.

I was lucky to be at Royal Ascot at all. Four months after joining the *Life*, my life almost came to an end. I was driving down to Somerset to interview Martin Pipe, the champion jumps trainer. I was late. I don't like being late.

A few miles from Nicholashayne, speeding along an empty lane, I picked up the map and glanced down at it, to check my route; glanced up, then glanced down, at 65 m.p.h. When I glanced up again, I noticed a terrible change. The road ahead wasn't clear any more. A bus had stopped to turn right. The cars behind it had stopped in sympathy. The last one in the queue was two cricket pitches away. I slammed on the brakes and thanked the car for braking straight, but knew there was no way I could stop in time. Cars were coming in the opposite direction and, on my left, there was a bank. The only choice open to me was whether to hit the car in front square on, or at an angle. I decided to hit it square on.

Time slows down, your senses become acute and focused, cutting out everything else; tiny actions unfold in a series of still frames. I remember making minor adjustments so that the front of my car was square against the back of the one in front. There was a tremendous bang. Pieces of metal trim and glass flew, clattered and scraped across the road. I was flung forwards and backwards. If I hadn't been wearing a seat belt, I would have been fired through the windscreen into the nearest mortuary. I was sure the engine would be pushed back into the car and crush my legs. It wasn't. That little Nissan Micra was wonderful. It was dead, but I was alive.

There was complete silence, and then time gradually rediscovered its old pace. I thought of petrol, staggered out and sat on the bank. The car in front was a write-off and, like me, the man in the car had suffered whiplash injuries. He was amazingly forgiving. His car had been pushed into the car in front, and that was damaged, too. He was less forgiving.

Eventually, I arrived at Pipe's in a recovery lorry. I didn't feel too bad, as long as I didn't do anything silly, like try to move. By the following morning, I could barely get out of bed. Putting my socks on was out of the question.

Visiting Pipe's yard was an eye-opening experience. Two days at Nicholashayne were enough to satisfy me that Pipe was a Newmarket straight ahead of most trainers, and that the rumbling criticisms of him said more about his critics than about Pipe. The whispered rumours and malicious gossip, of dark deeds in the laboratory, of horses worked cruelly hard, were ignorant nonsense, circulated by less able trainers and given currency by small-minded envy. People could not accept that Pipe was able to improve horses to the extent that he sometimes did, without resorting to malpractice; but he could, and did.

Pipe wasn't a particularly clever man, and didn't claim to be, but he recognised the importance of constantly asking the question, why? Why are things done this way? Is this the best way of doing them? Often, there wasn't a satisfactory answer, and Pipe set out in search of one, armed with an open mind.

Pipe thought about what he was doing, and organised himself and his team to do it. When I watched his string working up the single five-and-a-half-furlong uphill woodchip gallop, the idle chatter about overworked horses seemed laughable. Pipe used the interval training method. The horses worked in groups of two and three, slow ones paired with slow ones, quick ones with quick ones. They would usually do three pieces of work, the first very steady, the second a bit faster, the third faster still, hacking gently back to the bottom of the gallop after each piece of work. They were never worked off the bridle, or raced against each other, and their work riders weren't allowed to carry whips.

On the gallops, and in their boxes, the horses looked relaxed, content and fit. If Pipe had a golden rule, it was that horses should be sent to the racecourse fit to do their job. They should be healthy, physically fit, and well schooled – and running in the right race. He didn't get them fit by working them to death, but by a considered regime which embraced swimming, and cantering indoors, and a horsewalker, as well as interval training. They were schooled, often, over fences designed to replicate the ones they would meet in real life, including open ditches. As their training progressed, their condition was monitored by regular blood testing. If, when they were about to race, a blood test cast doubts on their well-being, they didn't run. When they ran, they often ran from the front. When Pipe asked why jockeys seemed happy to sacrifice ground at the start, and to hold their mounts up even when the pace was unhelpfully slow, he didn't get a satisfactory answer, so he usually advised his jockeys to make the running.

Pipe has had a unique influence on the way in which horses are trained in Britain. It goes beyond the fact that many trainers acknowledge having adopted elements of his approach. Pipe has contributed to a climate in which trainers question their own methods, and actively seek better ways of doing things in the hope of gaining an edge over their rivals. Yet, for all the records he has broken, and the flattery of imitation, Pipe is doomed to attract respect rather than affection. A lot of leading jump trainers are sociable extroverts who project themselves on to the stage, like David Nicholson and Jenny Pitman; or clubbable members of the Lambourn fraternity, like Kim Bailey, Nicky Henderson and Oliver Sherwood. Pipe is a very different personality. He would not feel comfortable in their club, nor easily be accepted into it.

For a long time, Pipe contributed a weekly column to the *Sporting Life* and, once a week, I drove down to Nicholashayne to work with him on it. As Pipe himself acknowledged, he was not very good at dealing with the press, tending to come across as defensive and unhelpful. Later, he made a serious and largely successful effort to improve relations; and at home he revealed a different side, relaxed and full of jokes (some of them pretty awful).

Some facets of Pipe's personality were alien to me, although they contributed to his success. For Pipe, training winners and making money were powerful motivators, and he was unsentimental about the horses he trained; not uncaring, but unromantic. His success put him in situations he didn't relish, although he welcomed the recognition and the business opportunities that came with it. I think he would have liked to have been left to get on with the task of training winners, undisturbed. We are all victims of our own personalities and, somehow, even when he stands in the centre, Pipe remains on the outside.

In 1991 I started a weekly column in the *Racing Times*, America's recently launched rival to the *Daily Racing Form*, and at the end of the year I went to New York, for the first time since 1968.

I spent most of a fortnight ill in bed or feeling ill out of one, which wasn't how I remembered New York, and may have coloured the experience. My nose watched Brooklyn through a handkerchief. When that handkerchief was too disgusting to touch, my nose viewed Brooklyn through another one.

The New York bars were good, and the pool in the bars was good, and complaining about being ill was quite good, but the betting shops were bloody awful. Outside were big signs reading Off-Track Betting, and inside other signs said No Smoking and No Loitering. There was a sign about AIDS, and another one inviting people with a gambling problem to phone the National Council on Problem Gambling Inc. No one seemed to be getting AIDS or phoning the Council, but nearly everyone was doing the other things.

There wasn't much else to do. No papers on the walls, no pictures on the television screens, no commentary worth the name. New York's OTBs reminded me of betting shops in Britain in the 1960s, except that most of the punters were either black or hispanic.

There were about sixty punters in one OTB I went into on the edge of Greenwich Village, and I was the only one with a racing paper. The *Racing Times* and *Daily Racing Form* each cost $2.50, which was $2 more than most punters had got. The form in the papers was full of strange phrases, like 'sat chilly', 'rated early', 'outbrushed late turn', 'put away speed', 'lugged in', and 'mud caulks'. After letting a couple of races drift by, I picked out Storm Fleet for the next. Storm Fleet had recently 'duelled inside, tired late, fog'. The other punters didn't call him Storm Fleet, they called him N. N finished second to A. One man came up to me and confided, 'I had the M horse.' 'I was lucky,' I told him, 'I had the N.' A pity I didn't have the A.

After that, I decided I'd better go to the real thing, at Aqueduct, so I got on the subway at Brooklyn and headed for Aqueduct racetrack. I did that several times. As the train rumbled along through Clinton-Washington, Franklin Avenue and Nostrand Avenue, it dawned on me that, although there were a lot of people on the train, I was the only white one. It was a strange feeling, very unlike the Piccadilly line, and I avoided other people's gaze, for fear that they might notice. Maybe I wasn't white any more, maybe travelling through Bedford-Stuyvesant had made me go black, and I didn't even know it.

Every journey, every few minutes, a beggar appeared on the train, begging. Sometimes the beggar didn't look drugged up, but usually he did. Often, he looked as if he would be very offended if you didn't give him everything you'd got which had 'In God We Trust' printed on it. I don't think God used the A train to Aqueduct. It is not one of the Great Railways of the World; it is not even one of the great subways of New York; but it does end up at Aqueduct, where it was cold and grey and I wandered around the huge aircraft-hangar grandstand and watched people, and listened. There's something about the way Americans talk that's always appealed to me.

A group of middle-aged men were post-morteming the previous day's racing before they got their teeth into today's card, which they would do as soon as they'd taken their teeth out of the burgers they were stretching their lips around and dribbling down their check shirts.

'The guy's the biggest stiff in the game. He jumped off it in the gates. The boys told him they didn't want this one in.'

'He takes them out of claimers and they improve ten lengths. No one can do that. It's got to be illegals. They're on juices.'

They needed to be, by the look of them; crocks, wheeled out to fill the thirty-eighth day of Aqueduct's winter meeting. All the decent horses had finished for the year, or gone to Florida or California for the winter.

'The horses are sore, and they're goin' to get sorer,' a man told me. 'I would give them away, but these guys put them together with spit and keep cranking away with them.'

During the races, not a horse's name was heard. Instead, punters shouted the numbers home, which came as a shock, to start with.

'Save that ground, seven, that's right. I'm seeing seven, where's that five?' The shouts of an exacta man, looking for the straight forecast.

Number seven was led into the deserted winner's enclosure. There were no spectators to witness the brief celebration, and the pressmen never left the cosy comfort of the press room at the top of the stand, where they waited for information to be sent to them.

British race fans have a feeling for horses, they respect them, far more than American racegoers do. But Aqueduct was the track where Steve 'The Kid' Cauthen rode six winners in a day, three times, when he was seventeen. Imagine it.

I went back to the States two years later, for the Breeders' Cup, my idea of the best race day in the world, especially when it's at Santa Anita, California. I think it must have been a Californian I sat next to on the plane out. Just before we launched ourselves across the Atlantic, she took the pair of red socks they give you on Virgin flights and sprayed them with something. When she had finished spraying them, she wrapped one around her wrist and put the other across her forehead. After a while, she put them back in her bag, until we were about to land. Then she took them out again, sprayed them, wrapped one around her wrist and lay the other on her forehead. I didn't ask her why, since the most likely explanation was that it was something her psychotherapist in California had recommended. I just sat quietly, filling in the ridiculous green card they give you before they'll let you in to the US of A.

'Have you ever been found guilty of moral turpitude? Yes/
No.
'Are you involved in genocide? Yes/No.
'Are you a terrorist? Yes/No.'
I wonder where the US Immigration Service stands on genocide. Do they see it, on the whole, as a good thing, or a bad
thing? How much genocide are you allowed to bring in with
you? How many people admitting to genocide do they turn
away every year? I can understand the terrorist question,
though. If you answer 'No' but subsequently show yourself to
be a terrorist, it means they can charge you with having lied on
your green card.

Californians are supposed to be very health-conscious; but
when we drove from Los Angeles airport to our Pasadena hotel
we passed one big sign that said 'Fatburgers' and another,
nearby, that read 'Mortuary'. In the hotel, there was a TV
channel showing the top half of people's naked bodies being
very noisy. I was about to ring reception to ask if I could have
another set to put under the top one when I spotted a card on
the TV which said 'Pay-TV $7.95 a Movie.' I had just spent
$200 watching someone having her foot tickled, and you
couldn't even see her foot.

It's a strange place, America, but Santa Anita is a beautiful
one. If you get up with the early sun, and go to the racecourse,
you can see the flat sunlight slice across the track, drawing
your gaze away to the razor-backed San Gabriel mountains
that make Santa Anita what it is, a magnetic place for racing.
Thin palm trees, eighty feet high, with a mop of leaves at the
top. Flocks of birds and strange, unfamiliar, tropical plants
around the paddock.

In the corner of the track, where the training barns meet the
course, is Clocker's Corner, where people in baseball caps stand
with breakfast in their hand and shield their eyes as they stare
out in search of the big horses. I stood watching with Cotton

Tinsley. Leather-faced from twenty years' training in the West Coast sun, he pointed down the track. 'You can lose the race right there.' I'd already noticed. At Santa Anita, the turf track sits inside the dirt one, and the bend Cotton was pointing out was sharper than any British horse would have met in its life, even at Chester. The European horses would meet it going faster than they'd ever been before, and they wouldn't know what had hit them. You could go round that bend three off the rail, and say goodbye to your chance right there.

I love the easy-going, casual-seeming, Californian style. It makes you relax. Horses come and go on the track in brightly coloured bandages and bridles, their riders in leather chaps and jeans, some riding long and some short, some standing in their stirrups, some crouched low. At first, it seems chaotic, horses this way and that, some walking, some galloping; and then you begin to recognise an order, the informal rules.

The training barns are like a village in a spaghetti western. Row after row of low, green shacks shared by horses and horsemen, piles of hay, and cockerels pecking in the dusty streets between, where horses walk and stand, having their legs hosed down. Clint Eastwood could be round the next corner. 'Cuidado Con El Perro' reads the sign: Beware of the Dog. Everywhere in the racetrack village the signs are in Spanish, and the music and chatter in Mexican. Some of the men can speak English, but many can't.

'Twenty-four years here,' Antonio Lopez told me, the only one in his group comfortable with English. 'So many good things. I have been elsewhere; here, it is the greatest. There is nothing like Santa Anita. If you love horses.' Antonio shrugged his shoulders and smiled, 'We can't live without them.'

With the race day a couple of days off, I flew out from Glendale to see what Las Vegas was like. You fly across the

Mojave Desert which, when you're not used to America, comes as a shock in itself. The most advanced economy in the world, and there's a great big desert sitting there, doing nothing, which is what deserts do. For all I know, it's not the only one. And then you suddenly notice that someone has planted 20 million light bulbs and called them Las Vegas.

At Vegas, they've taken glitz and turned it into a city, a willing illusion. At exactly six o'clock, it doesn't really matter whether it's a.m. or p.m. a volcano erupts. The ground rumbles, burning gas shoots into the air and water itself seems to be on fire. At six-thirty, the volcano outside the Mirage erupts again, and at seven o'clock it will erupt again. Further down the strip, a full-size pirate ship is being attacked by a seventeenth-century police boat. The attack is inconclusive; they relaunch it half an hour later, and half an hour after that.

The volcano cost $150 million to build. In America, they like to tell you things like that: how big a deal was, how much a car cost, how much meat you are getting in a burger, how big they can make your breasts, how much it's going to cost you if you want to build a volcano. As I walked past Cleopatra's barge, and a flashing sign in Caesar's Palace which announced 'Megabucks $7,826,159,' a man handed me a brochure. 'Brothel Tours Inc. Brothel Tour Vehicles Are Despatched At 2.30 p.m., 6.30 p.m., 10.30 p.m. and 2.30 a.m.' Everything has to be big. You can't even go to a brothel on your own, you have to make up a coach party.

Back in Pasadena for Breeders' Cup Day, I got to the racecourse at 8.30 a.m. You might think it would have been deserted. It wasn't. By 9.30, there was a queue 100 yards long for reserved seats, and race fans were already picking their Pick Six.

'Three bloody Marys and a screwdriver,' someone said to Mike, the showman barman on the first floor of a grandstand four furlongs long. 'You bet,' said Mike. This was his day, and he

181

was going to be remembered. 'Big glasses, gentlemen? Sure you do.'

Every country has its own way of talking the horses. 'Hey, Bob, watch out for that eight. Hey, listen to me, he's got the only speed. This guy goes wire to wire.'

'Thirty Slews won't win it. I saw his last two runs and they say that he couldn't beat a fat man.'

They're in the gate for the first. 'I'm worried about the eight, baby.' Then he stopped worrying and started screaming, and afterwards, when five had beaten eight, 'Hey, look at this. I did the exacta, eight and five. No quinella. Am I a goo-goo, or what?'

For the Americans, the race of the day was the Breeders' Cup Distaff, with the awesome foursome of Hollywood Wildcat, Sky Beauty, Dispute and Paseana. Paseana bidding to double-up on last year's win; Sky Beauty the East Coast Queen. Dispute never engaged the leaders and, as the field leaned into the home straight, Mike Smith, New York's champion, drove Sky Beauty up on the outside to make it a line of three with Hollywood Wildcat and Paseana. The East Coast spoiler couldn't sustain her effort, leaving Hollywood Wildcat and Paseana to battle to the wire, giving away nothing. A hundred yards out, Eddie Delahoussaye waved goodbye to his whip but Chris McCarron could still not quite force Paseana's flaring nostrils in front.

But we Europeans had been waiting for the Mile. Americans can seem insular. We wanted to make them take notice. We didn't want to hear a single American tell us that our horses were like our heavyweights, bums with their legs in the air. 'Hey, I'm saying something. Hey, hey, we're here too, you know. What d'ya think we are, then, bums?'

But there was Lure. Everything about that race was Lure. America's champion miler, winner of the race at Gulfstream Park in 1992. Lure was simply the best.

American trainers and jockeys are up-front; acquaintance is easy, even if friendship is harder. Take Shug (as in sugar) McGaughey (as in Magayhe), Lure's trainer. I wandered along to barn 24, one of those small, low, green, wooden sheds with the only clue that it wasn't a pauper's shack the sign on the wall, 'Phipps Stable.' The Ogden Phipps dynasty was one of the most powerful in the United States. And there was Shug McGaughey, short, stubby, pugnacious, a college drop-out who started as a $40 a week hot-walker and pulled himself off the bottle. 'I would leave the barn at night,' Shug told me, 'to get away from it. That's what I drank for, to get out of the pressure.' It made me want to root for him. 'Lure's the one,' said Shug, 'he's awesome,' and I believed him, and Mike Smith said the same. 'If it is meant to be, if it is the Lord's will.' Funny, Americans, about religion.

The Lord didn't do Lure any favours in the draw. Since the first Breeders' Cup, in 1984, no horse had won the Mile with a stalls position higher than 10; Lure was drawn 12.

It gave him the chance to show his greatness. Smith had Lure matching strides from the gate with Wolfhound, forced to use Lure's speed to get a position into the first, hold-your-breath bend. Behind, Barathea didn't corner, sending horses outside him reeling towards the outside rail. Lure was bumped by Ski Paradise but Smith quickly rebalanced him and dominated from the front. When a horse uses early pace like that, you are looking for him to crack late on, but that was the measure of the horse; Lure never cracked. 'The undisputed mile champion of the world. Back-to-back Breeders' Cup Miles,' said the announcer. 'Yes, sir.'

It wasn't nationalism that made me want Europe to win the Turf or the Classic. If we didn't win a thing, would we give beautiful Santa Anita a miss next time? And the 'take no notice of the European runners' attitude of many American race fans was irritating. Hey, these are good horses. Intrepidity, Opera

House, Apple Tree, Hatoof, Hernando, in the Turf. We know many things are against us, but we came, we had the bottle. We don't see you in Europe, taking us on there. You're home boys.

But when they hit the quarter pole, it was Kotashaan and Bien Bien, the local heroes, the fans were shouting home. We were on the sidelines, not counting.

There was just the Breeders' Cup Classic left. Three million dollars to the winner, on the dirt. If only Ezzoud or Arcangues could sneak a place, but it wasn't likely.

Then it happened. 'Oh, my God. It's a freak show,' shouted the man in a white baseball cap, while the crowd hummed in disbelief. Arcangues. It was eerily quiet. Around me, people peered into their *Daily Racing Form* for an explanation, a clue. They couldn't find one. 'It's only won one race in its life,' someone said. That wasn't true; Arcangues had won four out of fifteen. Then the dividend flashed up on the screen in the infield and everybody gasped and turned to their neighbour – $269.20 for a $2 stake.

'Boy, we cream them on the grass, then they do this to us on the dirt.' Yeah, we needed that.

It made me want to go back again; and the following year I went via Melbourne, and the Melbourne Cup.

The sense of good fortune has never left me. To have the chance to watch racing in France and Ireland, Germany, Italy and Sweden, the United States and Australia, even Dubai, seems extraordinary to me.

Melbourne Cup day is how a big race day ought to be, a great knees-up. I flew into the airport without a visa, but it didn't matter, because I was there for the Melbourne Cup.

'Just fill in this form, you'll be right. What do you know about it this year?'

I didn't know that when I walked through the gate at Flemington racecourse, the first thing I'd see would be an elegantly dressed lady standing with a gorilla, who was looking at a group of girls dressed as nuns, with short black skirts. Also a heavily tattooed man, in a lemon ballet skirt, white bra and yellow shoes. His girlfriend had a bale of straw on her head.

The weather forecast said it was going to rain, but they watered the course anyway, and then it did rain. While it was raining, 250 men in kilts and musical instruments marched up and down the track. Seventy-five thousand Australians, men, women and others, were going to have a bloody good time even if the Lord, in his infinite wisdom, decided to chuck it down, which he did.

I had already had my first winning bet in Australia, in the eighth race on Victoria Derby Day: $50 on Starstruck, at 7–2. Post-race euphoria was building up nicely, when they announced what they call a protest. Mark Miller, Starstruck's rider, had committed a minor infringement. He had stuck his elbow into Alf Matthews' face. The stewards didn't bother to ask my opinion, threw out Starstruck and suspended Miller for a month. At least it meant I could keep the ticket.

Jeune won the Melbourne Cup, and then I flew to Louisville, Kentucky, to watch the Breeders' Cup at nearby Churchill Downs. I love those names. Looevill, on the banks of the O-hi-o. 'How ya doin there?' I like the way they fill those big cartons full of ice, ready for your Diet Pepsi, and I like the way they put a napkin on the bar, ready for you to dribble your beer on to.

'You'd better be careful of the women,' a cab driver told us, encouragingly.

'Why's that?'

'Traaansveestites,' he said, through his one front tooth.

'All of them?'

'Nineteefarve per cent. If ar evva geet treeked bar one, ar promise u, ar'm goin ta put mar gun ter mar head, an blow mar brains straight out.' He nodded. 'Yes, sir.'

Ninety-five per cent of the cab drivers in Louisville are ninety-five per cent mad.

In Zeno's, one of those bars that you wouldn't want to go in when you look inside but feel fine once you're in there, they had a big, fat, bearded blues harmonica player. They also had a man in a dinner jacket and red bow tie who had been delivered in a stretch limo and would be collected in the same way. He played a couple of games of pool, lost his temper a couple of times, then left.

'Who was he?'

'Local millionaire,' said the barman. 'Never had to do a day's work in his life. Got so much money, doesn't know what to do with it, except be an asshole.'

A small, black woman danced solo to the fat harmonica player while, over the road, in Tiffany's, women took their clothes off, made love to a pole, and then got men to buy them a 7-Up for $32, in the pathetic, vain hope.

You couldn't even be sure it was $32, because $1 bills look the same as $20 bills, and they look just the same as $100 bills. You think you've tipped room service $1 for bringing the coffee, and then the man bursts into a broad grin and says, 'Well, thank you, sir, that's mighty kind, I'm sure. Have a nice day, now.' And you've just paid $50 for an espresso.

Back in Zeno's, the fat man's harmonica wails out, 'I was born under a bad sign, I been down since I began to crawl, if it wasn't for bad luck, man, I wouldn't have no luck at all.'

At the track, a man told me, in the way that punters the world over can't resist telling other punters, that, the previous year, someone had put Arcangues' number down in his Pick 7, by mistake, and couldn't be bothered to change it. He won $1.5 million. I like that.

At Churchill Downs, Gladys Knight sang 'The Star Spangled Banner'. 'The land of the free, and the home of the brave,' only she sang it slower than that. And the crowd applauded. They're like that in America: patriotic and proud and want to show they're the best, and think they are. Probably they don't think

186

like that in inner-city slums and black ghettoes, but they do in the grandstand at Churchill Downs on Breeders' Cup Day.

Barathea, honest and reliable and talented, but a bad luck horse, won the Breeders' Cup Mile, and Frankie Dettori executed his circus ring dismount just in case someone hadn't noticed who had won.

In Britain, foreign runners arouse interest; in the States, puzzlement and mild concern. The crowd goes quiet, as if something has gone wrong with the natural order of things. It was the same after Pat Day had ridden a hare-brained race on Paradise Creek to get beaten by Tikkanen, representing France, in the Turf. While Mike Smith waited patiently, fourteenth of fourteen, on Tikkanen, Day allowed Paradise Creek, on his first venture over the mile-and-a-half trip, to stride along at track record-breaking pace. You don't do that, but Day did, and killed his mount off in mid-stretch.

Dettori was the only British jockey who matched the Americans for projecting himself, and he isn't British, although that's how we like to think of him. When Frankie's father, Gianfranco, was twenty, he got on a boat in Sardinia and set off for Milan, where he got a job in a restaurant. One day, Gianfranco's boss said, 'Franco, look at your shape, you should be a jockey.' Gianfranco, short and stocky, and wanting to make something of his life, caught a train to Rome, taking a packet of cigarettes and a case of clothes, went to Capannelle, to the stables of Vittorio San Marzano, and asked for a job. He had never seen a racehorse, never sat on any sort of horse.

Every day, for six months, he swept the stables and forked manure. In the stable next to one of the ones Gianfranco cleaned was a crazy horse. When they exercised him, the staff gathered to watch, for the day's entertainment. One day, the lad who looked after the crazy horse didn't arrive. The horse stood in his box. The next day, again the lad didn't turn up. Gianfranco said to his boss, 'I will ride him, let me ride him.'

Vittorio San Marzano laughed and the crazy horse, that no one wanted to ride, stayed in his box.

But the next day the trainer wanted the horse exercised, and the lad still hadn't come back. 'All right, Franco,' he said, 'you have your way, you can ride him.' So the stable staff gathered to watch Franco ride the crazy horse, who had stood in his box for three days. The exercise gallop circled the yard and Vittorio reasoned that, if Franco stayed on, the horse would just gallop round and round until he decided to stop. That would be all right.

The crazy horse, that no one could hold, cantered steadily round, twice, then calmly came to a halt. No one could believe their eyes. 'You had better ride him at the races,' said Vittorio. In 1961, at Capannelle, outside Rome, Gianfranco Dettori rode his first winner, on the crazy horse.

When I visited Capannelle, Dettori's son, who loves and is proud of his father, pointed up at a big, autographed picture in the jockeys' room. It was a picture of Gianfranco riding Wollow to victory in the 1976 Two Thousand Guineas at Newmarket.

'My father met my mother at the circus,' said Frankie, 'and they produced a clown,' and he laughed.

Pat Eddery, that day at the Curragh, just said, in his laconic way, 'He's a very nice horse.'

The night before that, in Dublin, we went to a Cajun cafe in the part of the young city where they have that sort of thing. I asked for jambalaya, because I like saying it. 'Jambalaya.' It's one of those words, like 'gumbo', which I thought was a swamp outside New Orleans, but turned out to be onion soup. 'Jambalaya, please, and a spot of gumbo. Make that two jambalayas, and go easy on the gumbo.'

The next day, Budweiser Irish Derby Day, was baking hot. Jack Doyle, the legendary bloodstock agent, was one of the few watching as the first of the Derby runners walked into the small pre-parade ring, tucked away at the far end of the main ring. Craggy face, striped shirt, wide red braces with big white spots, a big, genuine smile, firm handshake, rough hands. I asked Jack what he thought. 'It's between the two,' he said. 'Maybe Desert Team could go well.' Then he shook his head. No point pretending. 'It's a match.'

There's always a nagging doubt in your mind when giants clash. One of them may have shrunk; the other may beat a tiddler. Hernando, the French Derby winner, was the first of the two to walk around the pre-parade ring. 'Nicely balanced,' said Jack. 'Not too big, a nice size. He looks really well.' Then Commander In Chief, winner of the English Derby. Jack's eyes narrowed, buried in ageing skin. 'He looks well. Yes, he's big, but not too big. They both look well.'

In the quadrangle of the bookmakers' ring, clerks sat at their high desks, like characters in a Charles Dickens novel.

'You wouldn't know which one to back, would you?' said one punter. 'It's a tough business, oh God it is.' Seven to four on the Commander, nine to four the French horse.

As the field hit the straight, the crowd roared. It roared again as Commander In Chief struck for home. It had started; the test had begun. Could Hernando keep his sting? Could Pat Eddery draw it? That was what the race was all about. All great races have a question like that in them. Eddery's whip went up, but it was only to press the question harder. Cash Asmussen, on Hernando, started to move. They were the only two. The race that had been billed as a match became a match. Asmussen's whip went up, and it meant more. Hernando had quickened to challenge, but he couldn't quicken again, and he needed to. Suddenly, you knew what the result was, and all that was left was watching it, but Asmussen kept going, because he knew he was in a contest that had to be played out to the end. Three-quarters of a length.

'He's a very nice horse,' said Eddery. Then he realised a bit more was needed. 'He's a very good horse. He took the speed off the other horse.'

I had a bet in the Dunnes Stores Ladies Derby, on Tbaareeh, who finished second, and then set off for the airport, where they gave us all tickets with numbers on. Mine was number 13. You got a seat if your number was less than 11.

At 11.00 p.m., we boarded a replacement plane for the replacement which hadn't arrived at 9.30 p.m. It had propellers and 'Amy Johnson' painted on the side. After it had chugged into Heathrow, Mr Mangan told me that they'd lost my suitcase, and gave me a card with 'Baggage Tracing Office' printed on it. He asked me to give him a ring in the morning.

'It is the morning,' I said. 'Do you mind if I ring you now, and get it over with?'

Outside, the notice on the concrete pillar said, 'After midnight, phone this number for the coach service to the long-stay car park.' It was an answerphone.

## *Chapter Twelve*

# The Most Dangerous Woman in the World

Not long after I had started writing a weekly column for the *Sporting Life*, a reader sent me a home-made postcard. It was square-shaped, with a photograph of a gorilla on the front. The gorilla's head had been cut out, and replaced by mine. The gorilla, who was better-looking, had his hand over my mouth. Above the picture, the correspondent had written, 'Some people think David Ashworth should keep his f—g mouth shut.'

I'm glad he wasn't talking about me. I sometimes think most of the *Sporting Life*'s readers are barmy; at least, most of the ones who get in touch. One man rang up to let me know that David Elsworth's horses were being hypnotised, while a woman wrote to tell me that she read me naked in bed and would I like to have a bath with her? I should have said yes, partly because it was the last offer I got and partly because, since the bath tiles started falling off the wall above the bath, I keep worrying that one's going to fall off and split my head open.

There's something about women and betting. It's not just that half-indecent ones don't go into betting shops, apart from the bookie's daughter in that little shop at the end of New Road in North Ascot, where Mart and I used to go just to watch her bottom when she turned round to put the prices on the board; and her top, when she turned round again.

A woman wrote to me once to explain that she didn't go into betting shops because, although she felt all right at a race-course, in a betting shop she felt like 'a kipper in a cattery'. I can understand that, but that's not the only reason. There's something else. 'When a woman bets and loses,' another female rarity wrote, 'she thinks, I wish I'd spent the money on a blouse. When a man bets and loses, he thinks, I knew I should have backed the second favourite.'

Sooner or later, women always say, 'Why don't you just have a pound on it?' They never say, 'Go on, stick two hundred quid on it and, if it wins, you can have me as well.'

I used to think it was something to do with their purses. It's impossible to be a gambler if you keep your money in a purse. South London Linda didn't have a purse. Men with purses are worse. Every time they take their purse out, which isn't often, they start talking about pensions.

Is it because women are too busy working and bringing up their children and their husband (much the same thing)? Have they got better things to do than spend all afternoon losing money? Is it because somebody's got to be sensible, and it's obviously not going to be him? Or have they been reading *Cosmopolitan* again and are going to need all the energy they've got for the evening?

I'd like to meet a woman who punts like mad and isn't doing it just because she's depressed, like the rest of us. I want to see her walk up to a bookmaker at Windsor, pull a bundle of £20 notes out of her cleavage, and say, 'Four thousand to four hundred, Opera House.' And smile.

I'm sure Mrs Abercrombie has never plucked a wad of £20 notes, or even $20 bills, from her cleavage, although I might be wrong. Maybe she's pulled them out of her garter. But that's leaping the gun a bit.

In the fall of 1992, as Mrs Abercrombie would have put it, Alastair Down said something about Prescott having a horse coming up. If it had been anybody else, I'd have been able to resist, but Sir Mark Prescott was the trainer I'd always dreamed of having a horse with; Prescott and Arthur Jones. A quarter share in Quinsigmond was going to cost £2,000 which, by a neat coincidence, was £2,000 more than I possessed. After the first training bill, I dropped my trainer a note. 'Dear Sir Mark, Received your first bill. Please shoot Quinsigmond immediately.' From then on, training bills got paid first, come what may. The only reason I've still got a body is that I couldn't find anyone to buy it.

I first became aware of Prescott during the 1970s, largely because of the successful partnership he forged with Elain Mellor in lady riders' races. Prescott seemed to win a lot of races with horses of modest ability. Heave To, Dawn Review, and Herradura each won nine times; Mandalus and Marching On won thirteen apiece; and in 1980 Spindrifter won ten races in a row and thirteen in all to equal Nagwa's record for the most wins by a two-year-old. Best of all was Misty Halo. Between 1981 and 1985, Misty Halo won twenty-one of her forty-two races. Yet none of these horses possessed exceptional ability. Spindrifter was officially the equal ninety-fifth best two-year-old of his generation. Misty Halo won most of her races with an unexceptional Timeform rating of less than ninety. But what Prescott's horses lacked in ability, he made up for with meticulous planning and brilliant placing. Not one of Misty Halo's victories was gained in a handicap, a tribute to Prescott's mastery of the programme book.

When I visited Heath House for the first time, in the spring of 1989, the wall around the yard reminded me of the wall which once surrounded my grandmother's back yard, with pieces of glass set in it. Prescott relished his reputation for old-fashioned discipline, and when we went round the yard for evening stables a lad or lass stood silently at the head of each horse, while Prescott examined and inspected, and entertained.

'This one had three runs last year. Ran badly, poorly and dreadfully. It looks as if it's going to be Catterick, G. Duffield, low draw, big stick, pray for a miracle.'

Prescott told me the story of an assistant trainer, now a trainer, who arrived for work late. Prescott rebuked him. The next day, he was late again. The flame reached the end of Prescott's fuse, not a very long journey, and Prescott set off for the assistant's lodgings, intent on instilling in him the importance of punctuality. He knocked at the back door. There was no reply, but the kitchen window was open, so Sir Mark squeezed through the window, and filled the saucepan which stood invitingly on the draining board with cold water. He crept upstairs, edged open the bedroom door, and felt his bile rise at the sight of the gently slumbering occupant. The trainer emptied the saucepan over the culprit's head, but didn't recognise the head when it shot up from the pillow. He was in the wrong house.

I have heard some of Prescott's stories several times, but he tells them particularly well, and when other people are there there is a vicarious pleasure in the anticipation of their pleasure.

On that first visit, there were game birds in cages by the path to the house, and in pens on the grass in the centre of the yard. Pictures of fighting cocks hung on the walls of Heath House, next to relics of bullfights in France and Spain. I can't remember seeing any pictures of hares, but Prescott liked hare coursing, too. I regarded it as an activity roughly on a par with the practice of raising pheasants for the pleasure of shooting them. Prescott, who played a major part in the revival of coursing, liked to launch the case for the defence with a pre-emptive strike. Supporters of hare coursing were the conservationists; its opponents posed the real threat to hares. Hares were better off with coursing than without it, because it led people to conserve hare stocks, and to educate farmers not to shoot them or spray their fields with Gramoxone.

One of Prescott's favourite statistics related to Chippenham Park. During the ten years before coursing started there, 2,860 hares were killed in the annual shoot; during the following ten years, sixty-three hares were killed, and there was no shooting and no Gramoxone. Abolitionists would have been happier if the sixty-three unlucky hares had also been protected, and coursing, shooting and Gramoxone all banned, but Prescott is good at exploiting the irrationality of some critics. He argues that animal welfare groups should be focusing their attention on hare shoots, which allegedly kill 300,000 hares a year and leave an equal number wounded, instead of reserving their emotional outbursts for coursing, in which fewer than 300 hares a year are killed, and none wounded.

'There has never been a wounded hare in coursing. It's either dead or it's alive; and it's not ripped to bits, they are not marked. The hare screams if it is not killed outright and, to urban man, that is very shocking, but if you or I knew that, when we died, we would suffer for no more than forty seconds, we would be very grateful. In nature, to suffer for forty seconds is very short.

'If you want to ban it as morally wrong, fair enough, but don't think that you would be doing the hares a favour. The overall welfare of hares is better on a coursing estate than anywhere else.'

Even Prescott's persuasiveness would have struggled to get me to go to the Waterloo Cup, where the dogs are not muzzled, but I was persuaded to go to the big Irish meeting at Clonmel, where the dogs are muzzled. The hares are trained to scamper straight up the 580 yard course, which runs up the middle of

Clonmel racecourse. When they reach the top, they also reach an escape screen. The hare can get underneath it, the greyhounds can't.

Bookmakers stand on Kenyan tea chests in front of the grandstand; Stephen Little, one of the biggest rails bookmakers in Britain, among them, although not actually betting. Across to the right, at the start of the course, is a small, open-fronted hut. Two dogs are held on leashes. One wears a white collar, the other a red one. It is a knock-out competition, with punters betting on each course, and on the ultimate winner. Big Chief was favourite for the IR£10,000 to the winner Hotel Minella Derby, and Flashy Fair for the IR£10,000 Sporting Press Oaks. A run leads past the front of the hut, and the hare runs along it, in front of the dogs, and scurries up the hill. The dogs are 'slipped', and the course is on.

The greyhounds can run faster than the hare, but the hare can see behind it, and when the dogs bear down on their prey it turns sharply and destroys their rhythm. The dog which is nearest to the hare when the hare is first forced to turn, wins the course. That is the point of coursing. It has nothing to do with catching the hare, which escapes nineteen times out of twenty, to cheers from the crowd.

Sometimes, the dogs reach the hare and bowl it over. Muzzled, they can't bite it, and usually the hare gets up again and escapes. Occasionally, they pin it down. Three hares were killed during the two days I was there. It is not a sport based on killing hares, but hares are sometimes killed. Horse racing, you might say, if you were mischievous, is not a sport based on killing horses, but about 200 are killed on the racecourse each year.

If your conscience allows it, coursing quickly becomes absorbing, the excitement building up through each knock-out round. There is a nice balance between the need for speed and stamina. Each course saps the dogs' strength. If it is a long course, with the hare turning the dogs, and turning them again, dragging them this way and that, it can drain a dog's chance away. By the time the hare nears the escape screen, the dogs are struggling to make ground. As round follows round, the dogs need to be tough, as well as fast.

In the final of the Oaks, on the third day of the meeting, Percys Lady, a beautiful black mover, shot clear; but it was a long course and, although she didn't falter, Flashy Fair gritted on, edged her head in front, and the hare turned, the crowd roared, and the judge on horseback waved his red flag for Flashy Fair.

Big Chief had been knocked out in the quarter-finals by Rebel Blue, now favourite to beat Seven Of Us, but Seven Of Us had been strong through the rounds, looking stronger. Fast from the start, Rebel Blue put lengths between him and his rival, but suddenly the gap started to close and Seven Of Us powered closer, a big white brindle. The crowd glanced towards the hare, made quick calculations of how far to go, how wide the gap, then Seven Of Us stormed past and the hare turned and the bookmakers on the tea chests roared, 'Yes, yes, yes,' as the judge's red handkerchief waved the defeat of the favourite.

The next day there was a race meeting at Clonmel. It had rained, and rained, and kept on raining, until the cars were stuck in Powerstown Park car park and the going would have had English stewards back home in front of a fire, but the Irish officials took a quick look, and wallowed on. And so it came to pass that I had my first bet on a jumps race in Ireland, in the Redmonstown Maiden Hurdle, on Lucky Salute, at 8–1. He was always going as the eventual winner should, and when Charlie Swan kicked him clear between the last two hurdles I turned to my neighbour and said, 'He's won it.' I turned back just in time to see Lucky Salute dive to his left and crash through the wing of the final hurdle.

Back at Heath House, Prescott put a video in the video machine and prepared to take me through the finer points of bull-fighting, but chasing hares was enough for me, and I preferred to sit in the kitchen, watching the progress of the mould on the marmalade.

When I first visited Prescott's yard I believed him to be one of Britain's best trainers; now, I don't have any doubt about it. There may be other trainers as good, but I would take some persuading that there are any better. If the 'Sir' tempts anyone to imagine that Prescott merely plays at training, they don't know the man; a professional, and an enthusiast. He once told me, 'When I hear a trainer say, "Oh, hell, I've got to go to Pontefract tomorrow," I think, "How lucky." Can you imagine saying to someone fitting bolts in a factory in Dagenham, "Oh, hell, I've got to go racing at Pontefract tomorrow." How lucky can you be?'

It was well worth buying one of Quinsigimond's legs for the unfailingly interesting and entertaining visits to Newmarket that her leg brought with it. It was also hopelessly irresponsible; but without the irresponsibility, there wouldn't have been the leg, and without the leg, there wouldn't have been the experience.

Or Quinsigimond's four victories, which is four more than most racehorses manage. The second was at Carlisle, in June 1993. Gary Nutting and I went up by train; Josephine Abercrombie and Sir Mark Prescott went by plane. Quinsigimond and Time Honored went by lorry.

'Life is fun,' Mrs Abercrombie informed me early on in an early conversation. 'It's certainly better than the alternative.'

Josephine, five foot four, in her sixties, and one hell of a woman, was an only child, which was the right kind of child to be if your father was James Smith Abercrombie. Jim Abercrombie invented a device for capping 'blowing' oil wells. The industry showed its appreciation by making him one of the richest men in Texas, where they know how to be rich. As a young girl, Josephine looked gorgeous in the nice hat and white dress her mother had bought for her, but preferred to sit on a horse in her Levis. By the time she was seven, she was showing horses and, by the time she was older, she was winning prizes with them in Madison Square Garden.

Madison Square Garden is where boxers have traditionally gone in order to beat the hell out of each other, and Josephine was rather attracted by the idea. In 1938, while Hitler was sitting down to eat Austria, Miss Abercrombie's parents settled down in the train from Houston to New York, where Joe Louis was about to fight Max Schmelling. The journey took three days. When they arrived at Madison Square Garden, Josephine's mother sat down, arranged her skirt, looked up, and saw Schmelling lying on the floor. He was hooked, and so was Josephine. She spent her time listening to fights on the radio, and in 1951, while America was fighting in Korea, Josephine watched Sugar Ray Robinson fight in Paris. 'He was like a black panther,' she remembered, 'and drove round in a big purple Cadillac.'

Maybe that was why, for a while, Josephine turned her considerable energies to men. She was Mrs Hudson for a year, Mrs Segura for eighteen months, Mrs Robinson for six months, Mrs Ryan for a year and Mrs Bryan for ten years. I don't know what was special about Mr Bryan, but he was the last. 'There will be no husband number six,' she announced, leaving herself free to concentrate on racehorses and boxers.

In 1984 she went to the Montreal Olympics, sat through 435 bouts, and then returned to Houston and launched herself as a boxing promoter, a job normally reserved for particularly unpleasant men, like Bob Arum and Don King. Arum once described Mrs Abercrombie as 'the most dangerous woman in the world', a form of compliment Mrs Abercrombie repaid by describing Arum as 'the toughest. You have to watch everything with him.' And what about cuddly Don King, whose hair makes him look as if he's already been in the electric chair once? 'Well,' Josephine replied, looking at me with a raised eyebrow, 'we used to wave at each other and say, "Hi." '

Mrs Abercrombie had an unconventional approach to boxing. She sent her boxers to university and gave them lessons in etiquette. They may have got caught with a right, but they knew what a fish knife looked like. It was after losing her main venue in Houston that Josephine switched her devotion to thoroughbreds. Pin Oak Farm bred Touching Wood, the winner of the 1982 St Leger, and Sky Classic, the Canadian champion, later stood there.

But, now, Mrs Abercrombie was standing in the stand at Carlisle, watching Quinsigimond gallop clear in the BBC Radio Cumbria Claiming Stakes (Class F). We all shouted 'Go on George!', as if it made any difference to George (Duffield), then we kissed each other, and the trainer congratulated us, probably for having shouted 'Go on George' so well. We congratulated him, and then went down to the winner's enclosure to swell with pride, disbelief, relief and self-satisfaction, which is what you do if you are lucky enough to own a winning horse's leg.

After we'd wallowed in that for a while, Time Honoured, Mrs Abercrombie's horse, won the Rayophane Handicap, and we went through the same procedure as before. Then Mrs Abercrombie and Sir Mark Prescott got on their plane while Gary and I got on the 6.18 from Carlisle station. By the time we'd arrived at Euston, Gary was going out with a Russian physiotherapist from Glasgow. The language barrier was worrying him. 'I only know one Russian word,' he said, 'niet.'

'That's all right. I expect it's the only one she'll use.'

A couple of weeks earlier, returning from watching Quinsigimond on the gallops, I saw an enormous grey thing. Mrs Abercrombie owned it, and it was called Hasten To Add. According to Prescott, it was a horse. It was obvious to me that,

200

if they could find a jockey tall enough to get on him, Hasten To Add was a stone-bonking certainty for the 1988 Grand National. He had just won a maiden race at Southwell, and was about to run in a ladies' race at York. We exchanged a few words on the fabulous creature's future, but none of them was 'Cesarewitch', which was as it should be, since I subscribe to the view that the only information worth having isn't available.

By the morning of the Cesarewitch, the great grey hope had been backed down to an incredibly short 3–1. This was the real thing, just as Quinlan Terry had been the real thing when Prescott sent him out to win the 1988 Cambridgeshire. When Quinlan Terry returned to the yard, Prescott built a new swimming pool for him. If Hasten To Add had won the other leg of the autumn double, he would have been sent on a luxury cruise, while Ladbrokes were rounded up and marched off to the cleaners.

Two furlongs out, Hasten To Add was lobbing along, ears flopping, travelling like a dream, but he didn't quite have the maturity to get home, and Prescott and the boys, and Mrs Abercrombie, were left replaying the memory of what the big horse had looked like two furlongs from the finish.

In the yard, they called him 'Harry'. Harry threatened to be a heartbreak. On his first two outings as a four-year-old, he was beaten a neck in the Bessborough Handicap at Royal Ascot and a short head in the Northumberland Plate; and then he went to York, for the Tote Ebor. Sometimes, you really want a horse to win, even though you haven't backed it. At York, that day, I really wanted Hasten To Add to win, and so did the huge crowd. In the parade ring, the great grey looked magnetic, magnificent. Some trainers don't give much in the way of riding instructions; Prescott isn't one of them. So you knew that when George Duffield kicked, with more than two furlongs of the straight to go, the plan was being unveiled.

The whole race was about that moment. The training, the thinking. Would the kick carry Hasten To Add clear, give him enough of a cushion? Two lengths, three, but the agonising endings at Ascot and Newcastle heightened the tension. You glanced back at the scrubbing pack, looking for a spoilsport, and one emerged: Admiral's Well. For a moment, Hasten To Add faltered; and then the grey colossus stuck on again to hold the unwelcome challenger by half a length. The elation was wonderful, wallowing in the pleasure you knew the trainer and owner were feeling. You wanted to shout, well done, George, well done, Mark, well done, Josephine; for once, well done, God.

By then, it had become easier to pay the training bills, and then harder again. It became easier shortly before half past one on 9 January 1993. As I stood among the seriously hooked, in the betting hall at Sandown Park, staring up at the list of runners for the 1.20 at Warwick, I experienced bliss, a condition brought about by the conviction that a 16–1 shot is certain to finish in the first three. It was obvious that Suez Canal was going to finish second or third to Her Honour, the 5–1 on favourite for the Leasowes Hurdle. I was hoping for 16–1, but would have settled for 14–1. Suez Canal opened at 20–1.

There is, as I have said before, an important rule to be observed on these rare and wonderful occasions. Don't even think of backing the 20–1 shot for a place on the Tote. The place dividend will be pathetic. (It was. £1.90 for £1). You are better off backing it each way with the bookmakers, if they'll have you, and accepting that the win stake is there to keep up appearances.

I approached a bookmaker and asked for 20–1. They looked at the bet and made a phone call. There was no problem with the win part of the bet, they were pleased to tell me, but I could only have half the place stake, or starting price, or Tote odds. I said I'd wait and see what happened. Suez Canal went to 33–1.

I waited a bit longer, then went back, and said I'd take SP, please. They looked at the bet and made another phone call. Win only, sir, or Tote odds. So I put it on with another bookmaker, at 33–1, which was the price Suez Canal won at.

Two weeks later, Gary and I set off for Kempton. I was changing gear in Battersea, just outside an antique shop, when the clutch pedal became rooted to the floor. The car ended up in Bolingbroke Motors ('All Servicing And Repairs'), and we ended up in Ladbrokes. I warmed up by backing Indian Quest and Early Man, both at 15–2, both winners. After that, I walked to the blue Mercury telephone near the traffic lights and backed Coraco at 33–1. Usually, when you want to do that, someone comes off the phone a second too late for you to get on the winner of the 2.30 at Sedgefield, or a second too early for you to miss backing a loser in the 2.45 at Ludlow. Not at the Mercury phone in Battersea. It was a good phone, and Coraco was an even better winner.

In the evening, when we'd been to the Uxbridge Arms and moved on to the spaghetti, I went over the story for the tenth time, for the benefit of those who had only heard it nine times before. That is one of the joys of winning.

That and being able to buy a horse myself, something I'd always wanted to do. For some time, I'd thought a horse called Supertop, trained by Peter Harris, would be ideal for the races I had in mind; so, in February, I rang Harris and offered, I think, £8,000. The owner didn't want to sell the five-year-old, which was wise of her, because, when the new season started, Supertop promptly won two of his first three races.

So I started looking at claiming races in which, as the name suggests, horses are entered to be claimed for a given sum. The rules have now been changed, so that anyone who wishes to lodge a claim, including the current owner, is restricted to 'bidding' the published amount. If there is more than one claim, the successful claimant is drawn out of a hat. In 1993, the rules were different. The claiming price was a minimum. Claims could be lodged for any amount above that figure, and the highest claim won the horse.

I waited and looked and studied until finally, in June, I found the horse I had been waiting for: a three-year-old filly called Mysilv, running in the BBC Radio Nottingham Claiming Stakes, entered to be claimed for £5,000. Arthur Jones had a runner at Nottingham that day, so I asked him to put in a claim for me. It wasn't a lot above the claiming price. I think it was just over £6,000, which wasn't enough. Jack Fisher, who owned Mysilv, had put in a claim for £8,000.

I should have bid more. The bloodstock market is comically fickle and, four months later, after winning one of her next eight races, Mysilv fetched 27,000 guineas. Despatched to David Nicholson, she won six hurdle races in a row, culminating in a memorable victory in the Daily Express Triumph Hurdle at Cheltenham. She was then sold for 155,000 guineas and went on to win the Tote Gold Trophy at Newbury.

The one that got away.

Very soon after that, I was no longer in the market for race-horses. I was barely in the market for packets of plain crisps. Just when my appetite for betting was becoming jaded, spread betting galloped into view, like the cavalry, rushing to help the Indians massacre the settlers.

In July, the 122nd British Open was launched down the fairways of Sandwich. Sporting Index were betting on the winning score, quoting 276–277. If you thought the winner would complete his four rounds in less than 276, you 'sold' at 276, for so much per shot. If you expected him to need more than 277 shots, you 'bought' at 277. In eleven Open championships played at Sandwich, only one player, Bill Rogers, had ever finished under par, with a score of 276. The weather was the key, and our information was that it would be unplayably windy. We bought at 277. The sun shone, the wind took the week off, and Greg Norman posted four successive under-par rounds to break the Open record with a score of 267. I don't think a single player lost a ball, but we lost all ours.

A month later, I confidently waded into a match bet between Rainbow Lake and User Friendly, who were disputing the right to be called favourite for the Yorkshire Oaks. I thought Rainbow Lake would finish in front of User Friendly, and put my money where my big mouth was. It was a mistake. User Friendly ran pretty much as expected, a well beaten third, but Rainbow Lake didn't run as expected at all, toiling half a mile from home, eased down to finish a thrashed seventh of eight, twelve lengths behind User Friendly. Twelve times my stake vanished down the Knavesmire.

Briefly, I branched out into betting on starting prices. If you add up the prices of all the winners at a particular meeting, what will they come to? It's an interesting question, and one day at Fontwell I thought I knew the answer; they would come to less than fifty-three. They would have done if Master Comedy hadn't won the John Rogerson Memorial Trophy at 33–1, Woodlands Boy the Royal Veterinary College Trophy at 50–1, and Polish Rider the Amberley Novices' Hurdle (Divison Two), also at 50–1. In the end, the total came to 153, which was like backing a 100–1 loser; 100 times your stake.

I rounded things off nicely in October, when smarty-pants Chris Eubank fought nasty Nigel Benn. I didn't care who won, as long as it didn't go beyond the eighth round, because I'd sold the duration of the fight at twenty-four minutes. I went over to a friend's, but she told me there was a house ban on boxing, so I went back home and watched it there. I was looking for an early clash of heads. Eubank and Benn threw a tremendous number of punches, which was what I thought they'd do, but I thought some of them might land properly. None of them did. My hopes rose briefly in the fourth, when Eubank caught Benn

205

a beauty in the groin but, unfortunately, he was wearing a protector. Cissy.

So the next day, feeling depressed, I went to the casino and got into conversation with a strange woman who suddenly asked, 'Have you ever had Ecstasy?'

'Yes,' I replied, 'when Julio Mariner won the St Leger.'

I explained to her that I only played blackjack and, because it was beginning to bore me, I allowed myself £100 and played £20 a hand. I played beautifully for five hands before running out of money, and then she sat down and plonked a big pile of chips on the table. She stood on thirteen against a picture, stood on fourteen against an ace, took a card when she had fifteen against a six, and won £265. I made a mental note to throw *Million Dollar Blackjack* away as soon as I got home.

She offered to buy me a Chinese meal and, when we got there, ordered numbers 7, 9, 17, 19, 21 and 23, because they were the ones she always did at roulette. 'I knew they'd come up this evening,' she said. In fact, they didn't come up until the following morning.

What I needed to get out was a cracking accumulator. Las Meninas to win the One Thousand Guineas, Mister Baileys the Two Thousand, Erhaab the Derby, all going on to Ian Paisley to lead a united Ireland.

When Quinsigimond was sold, she fetched 28,000 guineas, twice what we had expected. I trimmed my share in our next purchase, Petomi, to an eighth. We spent a long time trying to discover who or what Quinsigimond was. She wasn't anyone, it was a made-up name. So was Petomi; made up from Peter and Tommy Mines, our partners in the partnership.

It's amazing, the names people give their horses. It first struck me when I was reading a report from Yarmouth, in 1968.

'The most astonishing thing about the race was the deplorable exhibition put up by the favourite, Karl Marx. He was labouring from the moment the tapes were released, dropped back from halfway, and finished last.' I'm not surprised, he must have been exhausted after *Das Kapital*. You sometimes have to remind yourself that you are looking at a horse, and not a Fireplace, Fridge, Spanner or Combine Harvester. Racehorses have been called Steelworks and Boot Polish and Launderette. One has been a Moth, and another a Porcupine, to go with the Vulture, Rhino, Kangaroo, Grasshopper, and Octopus.

.The winner of the 1975 Grand National, L'Escargot, evidently got his name because, when his racing career was over, the owner intended to eat him. He wasn't the only one. The Menu, prepared by The Chef for the Glutton (by Major Portion) was huge. You could start with Mussels and then move on to Cottage Pie with a Jacket Potato, Cauliflower and Broccoli. For pudding, there was Treacle Tart, Stilton and Black Coffee. Wash it all down with a drop of Frascati and settle back with a Small Scotch, with Snuff to follow. During the 1960s, I remember Spring Cabbage bolting in countless times, and he kept better than most vegetables, racing until he was thirteen. Oscar Wilde had trouble keeping up, but you'll remember that Bobby Moore led for a long way in the 1969 Champion Hurdle, before Persian War took over, while Henry Kissinger defied overweight to land the 1981 Mackeson Gold Cup. There is a long tradition of naming horses after exotic places – Tuscany, the Seychelles, Watford Gap and the M Twenty Five. Sometimes, the horse's name identifies its owner. For years, Guy Reed played cowboys and indians, with Warpath and Apache, Tomahawk and Cheyenne. Steven Astaire had a lovely line in Marx Brothers film characters, such as J Cheever Loophole, Syrus P Turntable, Hugo Z Hackenbush and Wolf J Flywheel, until he ran out of names. For a long time, Lady Beaverbrook used to give her horses seven-letter names, such as Relkino, Bustino, Niniski, Petoski and Boldboy, but there were notable exceptions, including Easter Sun and Minster Son.

Some of the wittiest names have been dreamt up at Louis Freedman's Cliveden Stud. In the 1970s, he owned two top-class fillies, full sisters by Reform out of Seventh Bride. Freedman called one Polygamy and the other One Over Parr. Catherine Parr was Henry VIII's sixth wife. I think that's the cleverest name I've come across.

It helps if you have the right sire or dam, and few have provided as much fun as Busted and Bustino. Owners tend to go down one of two routes. Route one leads to Going Broke, Overspent, or with an Overdraft, ending up in Queer Street. Route two means going Strapless (out of Dame Foolish). In France, one of Busted's progeny, out of Amazer, gloried in the name of Amazing Bust, while Toby Balding came close to matching that with Cleavage, whose dam was a Busted mare called Divided. I liked that.

There have always dubious names, if you cared to look for them, like Muff Diver, Who Gives A Donald and the notorious Selosra, a name which, in 1972, the Jockey Club ordered be changed. My own favourite is Entire, a gelding out of Tactless, but I also have a soft spot for Rhett Butler, by Bold Lad out of Pussy Galore.

Weatherbys employ staff to weed out doubtful submissions but some of them must have had a sheltered upbringing. In the 1960s, Joe Lisle had a lot of horses in training with Denys Smith. When Sixty Nine slipped through the net, Lisle quickly followed up with Soixante Neuf. Luckily, Soixante Neuf was a gelding. If he'd gone to stud, he might have had his own ideas about the game.

## Chapter Thirteen

# How to Win the Jackpot

Every punter has one story like this one. This is mine.

On Saturday 15 January 1994, the Tote Jackpot, which hadn't been won for several days, wasn't won again, which meant that £67,053.76 was carried forward to Lingfield's meeting on Tuesday 18 January. I thought I'd have a go at it, so, in the morning, I sat down, worked my way through the form for the six Jackpot races, and put biro blobs next to my selections, in the way I always used to. Then I added them up – 3 × 3 × 3 × 2 × 2 × 4. It came to 432 combinations. Should I or shouldn't I? No, it was too much. I'd better knock one out.

I thought of knocking Northern Conqueror out of the last but, in the end, I knocked Special Risk out of the first, which saved me £144, but cost me £44,000, which is what the Jackpot would have paid if another winning ticket had been added to the 1.38 successful ones. Special Risk won at 25–1, and I had the other five winners.

You'll have spotted two of my golden rules already; always do the Jackpot to the full £1 stake, and always have more selections in the sixth race than in any of the others. Experts will tell you that each race should be treated on its merits. The last race may only merit two selections; it may merit only one, a banker. That is the sort of nonsense you get from people who have never even gone close. They don't know what it feels like. If you go out in the first race, it's not too bad. You cry for a while, obviously, and complain bitterly, but you can get over it. It's not like that if you've had the first five winners. You're sick with worry. You realise, too late, that you should have included half the field in the last, all the field. What on earth were you thinking about?

The next rule is that you don't do it with anyone else. A lot of people do, and when I told Ian the sorry story he said that I should have given him a ring, and he'd have split it with me. It's true, he would have done, and we'd have won £22,000 each, but that isn't the point. The point is that, if someone suggests a joint effort, it must mean they think you are good; they respect your judgment. If you are so good, why would you want to do it with them? Either you'll pick a 33–1 winner, in which case they're going to get an unfair share of the winnings, or they'll pick a 33–1 winner, and start hinting that, really, they ought to have more than half of the £224,000.

No, the thing to do is to say, politely but firmly, 'No, thank you, I am perfectly capable of winning it on my own.' Don't be disheartened by repeated failure; it means that it will soon be your turn. Sometimes, five of your six selections will win, and the other one finish second. The rest of the time, all six will win, but you decided to do the Placepot, instead. It's a laugh, isn't it?

There is one important rule, as I discovered at Lingfield: never cross out a selection. When you've made your selections, and worked out how much it's going to cost, to the full £1, on your own, be positive. Don't say, 'Christ, £876!' Say, '£876. I wonder if that's enough? Maybe I'd better sell the car and put in a few more.' Which is what I did a year later, when the Jackpot reached a record £2 million, at a small jumps meeting at Exeter. The previous day, when it reached £1 million, I'd thrown my contribution in to the well and somehow felt that, if it was worth having a crack at £1 million, it was worth having a go at £2 million. So I did.

I was on floor 23 of Canary Wharf that day, which is similar to Beachy Head but with suicide-proof windows. As the winners built up, the *Life* staff offered their encouraging advice. I should have put Trevaylor in the 3.30; I'd made a big mistake leaving Dubit and Sorrel Hill out of the 4.00; Rich Life, who I didn't have, was going to win the last.

The turning point was when Rufus, who I had, beat Boogie Bopper, who I didn't have, by a short head. A short head. I tried to be philosophical. There were punters out there who would end the afternoon with five winners and Boogie Bopper. What were they going to feel like? I told myself how lucky I had been and that, whatever happened after Rufus's race, I had no reason to complain. But I would have complained; I'd have complained like mad. It would have been the only pleasure left.

For a while, between Rufus winning the photo-finish and Bluechipenterprise winning the hunter-chase, I thought I was going to have a coronary. I didn't know whether to sit down and have a heart attack at my desk, or stand in front of the television and wait for it there. In the end, I settled for pacing up and down, sweating a lot, and talking nonsense. At ten past four, at the age of forty-six, I suddenly discovered prudence, although it didn't do me any good, which is what I'd always suspected of prudence. I thought I'd better not risk having picked five winners and losing, so I rang Victor Chandler.

I'd included three horses in the last race, and I knew what I stood to win if Pongo Waring won (£11,993), or Beyond Our Reach (£13,135) or Chickabiddy (£20,608). Victor, one of the few proper bookmakers left, offered me a price against any of the others winning, and I put more than £5,000 on, to make sure that, whatever won, I won at least £2,500. Pongo Waring

211

won, and I looked forward with increased enthusiasm to watching Petomi make her reappearance as a three-year-old.

The previous year, as a two-year-old, she'd been ill. Most of Prescott's horses had been. They'd got the virus. He'd ring up, diligently, every Sunday morning, to tell me how ill she was, except when he was in France or Spain, watching bulls being killed. To begin with, Petomi was really quite ill. Later, she was hardly ill at all and, eventually, there was talk of her getting better. After a couple of months she started walking, and our telephone conversations moved on from scoping and bacteria and blood counts to the vexed question of whether we should stick to walking, which she was now quite good at, or risk the odd canter.

When Petomi was getting better, I went up to see her, and she walked out of her box very impressively, and back in again. 'She's grown, hasn't she?' I didn't know whether she'd grown or not but, since she hadn't done anything but eat for two months, it seemed a fairly safe bet. I patted her on the neck, which is what owners do, and said, 'Feeling better, then?' which is the sort of inane question owners ask their horses. She didn't reply, probably because she was feeling too ill.

You feel as if you've been properly initiated into ownership when your horse, or your half-leg of it, gets the virus. 'Oh, she's had the virus,' you say, and everybody nods knowingly and talks about great viruses they have known, and then moves on to the problems of rape seed and vaccinations.

Eventually, Prescott got Petomi to a racecourse, and within the space of a month she rattled off three victories, at Folkestone, Wolverhampton and Leicester. This was a testament not to Petomi's ability, which was distinctly limited, but to Prescott's skill at placing her.

Petomi's unbeaten record made her look better than she was. She was a small filly, unlikely to improve from two to three years of age, and we knew the time was right to sell her;

but, unfortunately, she developed a knee problem, so we kept her. Overrated by the handicapper, facing ground firmer than she liked, intermittently lame, Petomi was one more challenge to Prescott, and he loved it. Jealous of his reputation, he wanted to show that, if one more victory was possible, he would tease it out of her. In September 1995, the day came. On a handicap mark which made her eligible for a suitable conditions race, with a bit of helpful cut in the ground, Petomi set off for Leicester, and we set off with her: Tommy Mines, team leader and colour bearer, jumping like a jack-in-the-box; Jo Willis-Bund and Chris McGrath, her boyfriend, both nervously amused; Alastair Down, bustling between serious intent and farce. The plan was to land the gamble at Leicester on Monday, and run Petomi again in a similar race at Nottingham the next day. Leicester was the Christmas cake, Nottingham the marzipan.

It was only my third trip to Leicester. The first was in 1970, when fog forced the meeting's abandonment; the second in 1974, when Ian Carnaby had his biggest bet of the week's racing holiday, on Pablond, and it didn't win. Third time lucky.

I had decided that the time had come to have my last bet. The desire to bet had been ebbing away; and I decided to go out with a bang. What I should have realised was that Pablond had been trained by Peter Easterby. His brother Mick trained Maid O'Cannie. Aimed at the Ladbroke Ayr Silver Cup, Maid O'Cannie had missed the cut, and was at Leicester, instead; drawn nicely, and in blinkers for the first time that season. The right faces were backing Easterby's. The wrong faces were backing Petomi: ours.

Maid O'Cannie broke well in the middle. Petomi missed a beat at the start, as she often did, and George Duffield then edged her across towards the centre from her high draw. Inside the final two furlongs of the six-furlong race, Maid O'Cannie

213

was cruising, Steve Maloney biding his time before kicking for the finish. When he did, the response wasn't quite as expected, and he sent her on with his whip. Maid O'Cannie seemed so much bigger than Petomi, probably because she was, but Petomi, full of effort, came to challenge, drew alongside and, for a stride or two, looked as if she might get the better of the tussle. Then Maid O'Cannie stretched her neck out again and Petomi was beaten half a length.

It's not until later you think about the defeat, because there's the excitement of having been part of the race, part of the action. The plan had worked, but it hadn't worked, that was all. 'Good try,' said Prescott, 'beastly Mick Easterby.'

There was nothing of Petomi, and she looked to have had a hard race. Easterby intended to run Maid O'Cannie at Nottingham the next day and, although she would have to carry a 3lb penalty for winning, we thought the Leicester race would probably have taken more out of Petomi than out of her conqueror.

In the morning, Prescott phoned. Petomi was perky, we might as well give it a go. None of us could go to Nottingham that day. I'd shut up shop and, apart from a token bet by Alastair, none of her several owners had a penny on. Working at home, I nipped out and watched the race at Fred Honour's, my local betting shop. Petomi drifted from 7–2 to 8–1, and trotted up, small as a rat and twice as tough.

In Britain's betting shops, punters must have studied the result, and the prices, and wondered what had become of Maid O'Cannie, and why they hadn't backed Petomi each way at 8–1, and whether the yard had pulled a trick.

We were chuffed to bits: Prescott had managed to squeeze another race out of her, but there was no trick. Petomi had won, but the wrong way around. A month later, we sold Petomi at the Newmarket Sales for 6,200 guineas, to race in Italy. My career as an owner was over, for the time being, at least. At the same time, I stopped punting. The urge had deserted me. People say, 'Why don't you just have a small bet?' Because, then, it isn't a bet, it's a social activity.

There was still the problem of how to fill the restless gap. Maybe I could write something.

## *A selection of non-fiction from Headline*

| | | | |
|---|---|---|---|
| THE NEXT 500 YEARS | Adrian Berry | £7.99 | ☐ |
| FIGHT FOR THE TIGER | Michael Day | £7.99 | ☐ |
| LEFT FOOT FORWARD | Garry Nelson | £5.99 | ☐ |
| THE NATWEST PLAYFAIR CRICKET ANNUAL | Bill Frindall | £4.99 | ☐ |
| THE JACK THE RIPPER A–Z | Paul Begg, Martin Fido & Keith Skinner | £8.99 | ☐ |
| VEGETARIAN GRUB ON A GRANT | Cas Clarke | £5.99 | ☐ |
| PURE FRED | Rupert Fawcett | £6.99 | ☐ |
| THE SUPERNATURAL A–Z | James Randi | £6.99 | ☐ |
| ERIC CANTONA: MY STORY | Eric Cantona | £6.99 | ☐ |
| THE TRUTH IN THE LIGHT | Peter and Elizabeth Fenwick | £6.99 | ☐ |
| GOODBYE BAFANA | James Gregory | £6.99 | ☐ |
| MY OLD MAN AND THE SEA | Daniel Hayes and David Hayes | £5.99 | ☐ |

*All Headline books are available at your local bookshop or newsagent, or can be ordered direct from the publisher. Just tick the titles you want and fill in the form below. Prices and availability subject to change without notice.*

Headline Book Publishing, Cash Sales Department, Bookpoint, 39 Milton Park, Abingdon, OXON, OX14 4TD, UK. If you have a credit card you may order by telephone – 01235 400400.

Please enclose a cheque or postal order made payable to Bookpoint Ltd to the value of the cover price and allow the following for postage and packing:

UK & BFPO: £1.00 for the first book, 50p for the second book and 30p for each additional book ordered up to a maximum charge of £3.00.
OVERSEAS & EIRE: £2.00 for the first book, £1.00 for the second book and 50p for each additional book.

Name ................................................................................................

Address ............................................................................................

.........................................................................................................

.........................................................................................................

If you would prefer to pay by credit card, please complete:
Please debit my Visa/Access/Diner's Card/American Express (delete as applicable) card no:

| | | | | | | | | | | | | | | | | | | |
|---|---|---|---|---|---|---|---|---|---|---|---|---|---|---|---|---|---|---|

Signature ...................................................... Expiry Date...............